Jewelry of the Stars
Creations from Joseff of Hollywood

Joanne Dubbs Ball

1469 Morstein Road, West Chester, Pennsylvania 19380

This book is dedicated to the memory of Eugene Joseff, an artist, entrepreneur, and visionary, whose jewelry brought beauty, style, authenticity, and an aura of magic to the "silver screen," and to Joan Castle Joseff, who, with courage and unwavering determination, carried his dream forward.

Also by Joanne Dubbs Ball:
Costume Jewelers: The Golden Age of Design

Black and white stills are from the Joan Castle Joseff Collection, with special thanks to the film companies, both past and present, that made them possible.

Printed in the United States of America.
ISBN: 0-88740-294-1

We are interested in hearing from authors with book ideas on related topics.

Front jacket: Necklace and earrings of Egyptian-inspired design from Joseff's retail line.
Back jacket: Hollywood's stars with Joseff jewelry, from top, left to right, Olivia de Haviland, Barbara Stanwyck, Jean Parker, Evelyn Knapp, Tyrone Power, Ginger Rogers and Rita Hayworth.
Title page: Created by Joseff, this fantastic crown and scepter have graced the movie and television screens for many years, used time and time again, especially in museum scenes.

Published by Schiffer Publishing, Ltd.
1469 Morstein Road
West Chester, Pennsylvania 19380
Please write for a free catalog.
This book may be purchased from the publisher.
Please include $2.00 postage.
Try your bookstore first.

Contents

	Prologue	5
Scene I	Movies—The Beginning	7
Scene II	Enter Eugene Joseff	15
Scene III	Enter Joan Castle..........................	41
Scene IV	Movies—The Golden Years	69
Scene V	"Gone With The Wind"......................	103
Scene VI	A Family Gallery	113
Scene VII	Joseff Jewels for Everyone	123
Scene VIII	Carrying the Dream Forward	159
	Epilogue..................................	186
	Notes	187
	Bibliography	187
	Movies... Movies... Movies...	188
	Index	191

Shirley Temple regally oversees her kingdom—including the original crown and scepter from 1939's *The Little Princess.*

4

Prologue

Once upon a time, in a place called Hollywood, there dwelled an extraordinary sorcerer. His awesome powers were spoken of in hushed, and most respectful, whispers. For in the twinkling of an eye, he transported jewels of great splendor to the magic screens of the kingdom, so that all its subjects could see, before their very eyes, the adornments of kings and queens, pirates and princes, Ziegfeld stars and Southern belles.

His name was Eugene Joseff, soon known as Joseff of Hollywood, and he conveyed to that mystical screen magnificent jewels of wondrous authenticity. His followers became legion, for not only were these shimmering baubles coveted by the esteemed ones whose bodies they adorned, but subjects everywhere desired them! And so, in those special places where all gathered to acquire such embellishments, his skillful renditions could soon be found.

And it was thus that the magical aura of Joseff spread throughout the land. Eugene Joseff—creator of "Jewelry of the Stars."

Rudolph Valentino (Tony Dexter) portrays the Sheik in one of the many "scenes within a scene" from the Edward Small production *Valentino* for Columbia.

Scene I
Movies

The Beginning

However rudimentary their beginnings, that entertainment extravaganza we call the "movies" is generally acknowledged to be the brainchild of Thomas Edison, and in the early 1890s the first of these flickering "moving pictures" could only be viewed by peeking through crude, hand-cranked machines in penny arcades and similar entertainment emporiums throughout the United States.

Although an inventive genius, Edison wasn't forward thinking with regard to what he considered a "lesser light" amid his many other successful inventions. He felt that one customer at a time was adequate, especially once the pennies eager viewers deposited to "take a peek" began flowing freely into his coffers. But when imitators jumped on the bandwagon, trying to combine the elements of this new contraption with the principle of the Gay Nineties' "magic lanterns," Edison reluctantly agreed to broaden his scope and expand these tiny pictures into an art form designed for *group* instead of *individual* entertainment.

The flagship performance of these newly refined motion pictures took place on April 23, 1896 in the Koster and Bials' Music Hall in New York City. The *Times* reported:

> Next morning, an unusually bright light fell upon the screen. Then came into view two precious blond persons of the variety stage, in pink and blue dresses, doing the umbrella dance with commendable celerity. Their motions were all clearly defined![1]

Heady stuff indeed—and thus *real* movies were born!

By the time the 1890s drew to a close, these short, ever-changing vignettes occupied a rather inauspicious spot on the theatrical bill of fare of the popular vaudeville houses of the day, generally following the "live" performers that were the main attraction. But, as with any core idea of merit, there are always those not satisfied with the status quo who strive to refine and expand the horizons of a fledgling idea while most of their contemporaries are simply muttering, "Good enough." Fortunately, the history of motion pictures is no exception, for otherwise the novelty of these very crude initial efforts would have rapidly faded into oblivion!

If such had indeed happened, it's a sobering thought. No innocent Mary Pickford with long, blonde curls—no Charlie Chaplin with mustache and cane—no Clara Bow with kewpie doll mouth—no Rudolph Valentino to set hearts aflutter—no Greta Garbo with her haunting beauty—no Shirley Temple to tug at our heartstrings—no romance and visions of wealth to ease our tired bodies through the Great Depression—no Busby Berkley and kaleidoscopic dancing girls—no sophisticates like William Powell and Myrna Loy or glamour girls like Jean Harlow, Rita Hayworth and Marilyn Monroe—no tight-lipped Gary Cooper or rugged John Wayne—no cowboys and Indians—no gangsters and molls. And no Clark Gable and Vivian Leigh to bring Rhett and Scarlett to life before our very eyes. A monumental cultural happening would have failed to gain the momentum necessary to vault it into an honored place as one of the most influential entertainment mediums of the twentieth century.

The patterning of our mores, hopes, dreams, and aspirations, and our understanding of the realities of the world around us, of war and destruction as well as fantasy and gaiety, would have been startlingly altered without the magic of the movies. And these fledgling films touched on other realms, as well, with early pioneers venturing into decidedly risky territory, confronting issues of life and death, philosophy, and theology. Even mystical themes appeared in abundance, especially after World War I when audiences were eager to retreat from the hardships of the past to explanations of hope. "...what most of these...motion pictures suggested almost subliminally, was a reassuring continuity between life and afterlife, between generations."[2]

And so, the far-reaching repercussions of these "flickering images" on our own society, and eventually the world community, are akin to the slowly expanding ripples one sees when a pebble is tossed into a peaceful pool of shimmering water. They journey ever outward, perhaps as the galaxies of our universe once did. When we gaze heavenward to view this brilliant "light show," we call them stars—just like those glimmering stars of that other "light show," the ones that glowed on the *silver screen!*

Conceived in the eastern United States, then burgeoning with generations of past and present immigrants, and aspirations both realized and unfulfilled, it is perhaps no mere coincidence that the making of these movies initially occupied somewhat dreary surroundings. Pioneering companies like Biograph with its genius director D.W. Griffith, a poet who saw the potential in film and brought it to fruition, were headquartered in New York, as was Vitagraph. Some scenes from the early *Romeo and Juliet* were filmed in New York's Central Park; Edwin S. Porter's *The Great Train Robbery* was shot in the then open spaces of New Jersey. Even animation found a place in this new medium. The first cartoon-like film was *Gertie the Dinosaur,* drawn by Winsor McCoy and presented to the public in 1909! In a leap westward, Colonel William F. Selig moved his company from the confines of New York and environs to Chicago for the filming of *Roosevelt in Africa* in 1910.

It seems only fitting that by the early teens of the twentieth century this now "teenage" industry had migrated even farther west, where it was brought to full maturity in California, land of sunshine and bounty, open spaces and renewed opportunities, rather than the tenements and teeming thoroughfares that surrounded its conception.

The tiny suburb of Los Angeles that became the hub of California's movie industry was called Hollywood. Rarely has a name been better suited to its "product." The fit is so perfect that one can only marvel at it—and question whether the choice was somehow preordained! In fact, had it not been for the intervention of some real "wild West" antics, the history of the movies might have had a somewhat different outcome.

The story goes that in 1914 a newly-formed film company headed by Jesse Lasky, in partnership with Cecil B. DeMille and Sam Goldfish, whose name was later changed to Goldwyn, purchased the rights to Edwin Milton Royle's *The Squaw Man*. They cavalierly paid $15,000 for the screen rights, which took a lot of courage considering they had bankrolled their fledgling enterprise with a mere $20,000.

As Jesse Lasky's son recalled in his memoirs, "Wisdom would seem to have dictated a trip across the Hudson River to Fort Lee, New Jersey, where more sensible one- and two-reel Westerns were then being ground out."[3] Determined, however, to give this Western an edge over the rest, the trio decided that nothing short of complete authenticity would do, and settled on Flagstaff, Arizona as a good locale to shoot *The Squaw Man*. DeMille was dispatched to scout out the territory, while Lasky and Goldwyn stayed behind. However, when his train finally chugged into Flagstaff authenticity took on a whole new meaning. A range war between cattlemen and sheepmen was tearing the countryside apart, so DeMille wisely decided that risking being shot added more flavor to the surroundings than he'd bargained for and hopped the next train heading due West.

Later he dispatched a hasty telegram to Lasky that read, "Flagstaff no good for our purposes. Have proceeded to California. Want authority to rent barn in place called Hollywood for seventy-five dollars a month...."[4] Lasky mulled this one over long and hard and finally gave his half-hearted permission—providing the rental was on a month-by-month basis with no long term commitment. "On this economical note the most lavishly extravagant industry in history was launched in Hollywood. And with it: The Jesse Lasky Feature Play Company: One barn. One truck. One camera."[5]

And so, by a strange quirk of fate involving a real life "shoot-em-up," Flagstaff, Arizona came within a hairsbreadth of becoming top contender for the movie capital of the world. All things being relatively equal, the scales must surely tip in favor of Hollywood as we breathe a collective sigh of relief...for "Hooray for Flagstaff" (or Pasadena or Burbank, for that matter) just doesn't equal the thrill of tapping our feet to the boisterous, happy-go-lucky "Hooray for Hollywood"!

Although attempts had been made to incorporate sound with photographs long before Edison's breakthrough in moving pictures and prior to DeMille's pioneering trek to Hollywood, these experiments were unsatisfactory and generated little interest. Even D. W. Griffith had a sound accompaniment to a portion of 1921's *Dream Street*, but that too failed to move the process forward. However, the four Warner brothers put their faith—and money—into a Bell Laboratories' device that eventually refined *talking* pictures. Licensed in 1926 by Warner Brothers, through Western Electric Company, it was called the Vitaphone. John Barrymore's silent film *Don Juan* was the first to incorporate a musical score, and a year later Al Jolson sang and briefly spoke in *The Jazz Singer*.

The stage was finally set for full-length talkies, the first of which was 1928's *Lights of New York*. Sound swept through theatres like a whirlwind, as owners frantically converted their suddenly archaic equipment to the revolutionary "talkies." In the blinking of an eye, the fuzzy caterpillar had turned into a gossamer butterfly!

The early decades of the twentieth century had most decidedly catapulted the medium to the threshold of greatness and universal acceptance, but it was the advent of sound that created an "understanding" of sorts. Movies were carried across that somewhat bumpy but always tantalizing matrimonial threshold during the 1930s and, over the ensuing years, settled into a relationship between performer and audience that remains unique. For never again will such a set of circumstances be so precisely in place—a revolutionary form of entertainment was offered to a nation of individuals searching for their place in it, followed in frighteningly rapid order by the chaos of World War I, the devastation of the Great Depression, and the threat and eventual reality of yet another World War. The yearnings of the audience were met, if only for an instant in time, in darkened theatres where stark realism and fairy tale fantasies mixed with those dreams and were limited only by the depth of each individual's imagination.

As Albert Leventhal wrote in the preface to Paul Trent's *Those Fabulous Movies Years: The 1930s*:

> Escapism was the order of the day, and film-makers transported audiences to Shangri-La and the jungles of deepest Africa, to the drawing rooms of the very rich and the perils of the old West, to the burning of Atlanta and gangster hangouts, to the Land of Oz and the home of Dopey, Grumpy, Sneezy and their four companions.

These escapist qualities have always been, and will undoubtedly ever remain, in the eye of the beholder. Interestingly, they appear to be more exclusive to film than reading an exciting novel, or even attending a theatrical performance. Could it be that the darkness in which movies are viewed creates an intimacy and anonymity that enfolds the audience more securely into the on-screen action, as was delightfully portrayed in Woody Allen's *The Purple Rose of Cairo?*

In the nickelodeons of silent films, adults lost themselves in the romantic escapades of Mary Pickford and John Gilbert. Young lads, on the other hand, were enthralled with a different kind of hero. The caps that perched jauntily on their heads when they hurried to the ticket window, nickels clutched in sweaty palms, were later filled with freshly-roasted peanuts and rested securely in their laps! Alternately shelling and munching, eyes widened in awe, they envisioned themselves engaging in the swashbuckling heroics of Douglas Fairbanks, Sr., or the "down home" courage of Tom Mix.

Either way, it mattered not. Romance or adventure, it was all the same—an entry into other realms, far removed from those the housewife, the laborer, or the young boys and girls would step into when the house lights came up and they wended their way to the often grim surroundings that awaited them outside.

These feelings were poignantly expressed by an 80 year old woman who won a $25 prize in an early *Photoplay* movie magazine contest, when she wrote:

> Time goes on, and once the thought of life's evening filled me with dread.... Do I live with memories? No! Around the corner is a little movie house. Each night I wash and dry my dishes, put on my hat and make a bee-line for it. Within those two hours I satisfy not only the beauty and romance I have been denied, but also the beauty and romance denied to my mother and grandmother.[6]

Whether to amuse, delight, frighten, or even subtly educate, what transpired on those magic screens—from nickelodeons to early "talkies" to the more sophisticated films that followed—still demanded a certain authenticity. A medieval English king would look foolish in the robes of an Egyptian prince, an American shop girl wouldn't appear on-screen in the gown of a Victorian lady and, by the same token, a member of sixteenth century Italian aristocracy shouldn't have her throat adorned with a twentieth century necklace. But in a 1934 movie she did.

Enter Eugene Joseff....

The gaucho hat from *Valentino*, the 1951 film starring Anthony Dexter as Rudolph Valentino, takes its rightful place alongside the original belt from *The Sheik* which Joan Joseff purchased at auction and which occupies an honored place amid her movie treasures. Valentino's performance in this ground-breaking film gave the term *matinee idol* a whole new persona, and *The Sheik* a special niche in screen history!

Studio publicity releases for *The Sheik* contained this deathless prose: "She was trapped, powerless, defenseless...she realized fully whose arm was round (sic) hers and whose breast her head was resting on. What had happened to her? Quite suddenly she knew...that she loved him...had loved him for a long time, even when she thought she hated him...."[7]

On a less emotional note, Valentino inadvertently played the starring role in a jewelry fad—this time a male one! When his second wife Natasha Rambova, a mogul in fashion and advertising and actually Winifred Hudnut, stepdaughter of cosmetics tycoon Richard Hudnut, presented him with a slave bracelet, young men, and probably many who were not so young, slicked their hair to a patent leather shine and wore replicas of the bracelet over their own wrists, with high hopes for a rapturous reaction from females approaching the adulation being heaped on Valentino.

An article entitled "Woman and Love," which Valentino penned for Photoplay in the early 1920s, was filled with some very succinct and inflammatory observations, to wit:

"The most difficult thing in the world is to make a man love you when he sees you every day. The next is to make him remember that he has loved you when he no longer sees you at all."

"A love affair with a stupid woman is like a cold cup of coffee."

In commenting about the American woman in particular, he wrote:

"She knows all of the bad and none of the good about passion. She has seen everything, felt nothing. She arouses in me disgust."

He negated most of the above by then commenting, "I believe the most irresistible woman in the world is the woman who is madly in love with you."

(*Photoplay Treasury*, edited by Barbara Gelman, Crown, New York, 1972, pp. 97-99.)

Since, at the time of this article, the "madly in love with him" category encompassed a vast majority of the American female population, his disgust couldn't have been too overwhelming! Mr. Valentino was most fortunate to have found fame in the early decades of this century. With such views, his star would probably have burned not so brightly, if at all, in the latter decades!

These stills from the 1951 Columbia Pictures' film *Valentino,* starring Anthony Dexter and Eleanor Parker, recreate scenes from Rudolph Valentino's silent films. His original belt from the 1920s added authenticity (as seen in photo above). The gold mesh belt in photo at right was also worn by Tyrone Power eight years earlier in *The Rains Came.* The Valentino belt also appeared at Anthony Quinn's waist in 1947's *Sinbad the Sailor* (below).

Eugene Joseff and actress Kathleen Wilson look over Joseff's supply of chains and period pieces. He always kept on hand as much as fifty feet of chain to meet emergency studio orders. Note the orderly array of cigar boxes on the shelves, which contain countless buckles, jewels and novelties.

14

Scene II
Enter Eugene Joseff

Of Austrian heritage, Eugene Joseff was born on September 25, 1905, in Chicago. His parents gave him no middle name, which was prophetically appropriate, for in manhood Eugene's first name would also become superfluous. This first son was a mere toddler of fifteen months when he was joined by a loveable intruder—a brother James. Fifteen months may seem insignificant, but regardless, Eugene Joseff was always the "big brother" and pathfinder, and the two boys became inseparable.

Events just over the horizon would reveal the timing of Eugene Joseff's birth to be fortuitous, for his arrival shortly after the turn of this new century coincided with the ever-growing realization that movies, that "newfangled" entertainment medium, might indeed be more than a passing fancy. Actors—and would-be actors, producers, and directors—jumped on the bandwagon. As he grew to maturity, Eugene aspired to fill none of those niches, however—even though he probably could have done so quite adequately. Instead, he was destined to play his own unique role in this unfolding extravaganza. In the meantime, growing up in Chicago provided a background that would serve him well.

Raised in the Catholic faith, young Eugene must have presented an angelic picture when he raised his voice in song as a choir boy in Chicago's Loyola church. Angelic, yes...but with a devilish glint of mischief in his eyes! Blessed early on with an inquisitive mind, Joseff surely caused many a staid teacher, or nun, to wince with displeasure. Although probably an exaggeration, Joseff later claimed that he was "kicked out" of every school he attended. More than likely he was simply told to mend his maverick ways and "mainstream" a path through the school system!

One thing is certain. He questioned, questioned, questioned. Artistic but firmly rooted, Eugene Joseff wasn't reluctant to get his hands dirty, and his interest in metal work gained him an apprenticeship in a foundry. The experience solidified a deep-seated curiosity about the basics of jewelry design, and he soon found himself taking pieces apart, studying the techniques used, and then reassembling them, all the while experimenting with new ideas. This period in his life would prove invaluable when he later faced the challenge of producing the unusual and seemingly impossible in jewelry design and manufacture.

Since a weekly paycheck had to be his first consideration, Joseff's first venture into the business world led him to what was then the more secure domain of advertising. Brimming with ideas, he was undoubtedly "a natural," especially in a field that, in the 1920s, was just beginning to explore its potential. Nevertheless, this exposure to Chicago's advertising world would prove to be short-lived. The Depression had begun, and its domino effect was already taking its toll everywhere.

It was then that Joseff, to the lasting benefit of movie fans and jewelry lovers everywhere, made a fateful decision. While the rest of the country was just beginning to suffer under the pall of hard times, only the virgin area of California, with its fledgling businesses, seemed to hold some promise for new advertising possibilities, especially those related to the entertainment industry.

And so, both Eugene and James searched for a fresh start in the sun—and sometimes *fun*—of Los Angeles and Hollywood. It wasn't the first time the Joseff boys behaved more like twins than simply siblings. In fact, some years later when Jim married shortly after Eugene, their mother Betty remarked that Jim's behavior was simply true to pattern. "Why he even got all the childhood diseases, like measles, after Eugene did," so a "copycat" wedding didn't surprise her in the least! At that point, both sons probably thought it was just like a *mother* to compare measles to marriage, and to somehow make it sound quite logical, at that!

As the saying goes, Joseff took to the new and exciting California environment like a "fish to water." The untapped potential was enormous, especially for those willing to explore untrod paths. If ever an individual fit this criteria, it was Eugene Joseff. Nevertheless, while continuing to dabble in advertising, creating jewelry remained his overriding passion, and although the business got off to a shaky and sometimes discouraging start, Joseff of Hollywood actually had its tentative beginnings in 1930.

With his dynamic personality Joseff had no difficulty cementing friendships among many "bright lights" in Hollywood's inner circle. One of these, an equally charismatic fellow, was Walter Plunkett. Firmly established since 1926 as one of the premiere costume designers in the industry, Plunkett's accomplishments are awe-inspiring, culminating in over 300 movies throughout his career. Later fated to design the costumes for *Gone With the Wind*, his credits had already included such classics as the original *Cimmaron* in 1931, *Flying Down to Rio*, *Little Women*, and *Morning Glory* in 1933, and 1934's *The Gay Divorcee*.

When discussing these frequently unsung celluloid heroes who contribute so much to the ambiance of film, it's important to recognize that there is a complex difference between the countless details that need to be reproduced when the viewer is seeing a "moving picture" and the mental visualization of a scene via the written word. In film, the writers, producers, directors, costume and set designers are charged with a personal and professional obligation to strive for accuracy. As in any other venture of such proportions, they weren't always successful and, on rare occasions, they didn't particularly care! For instance, a Parisian love scene in the film *Paris* was illuminated by a moonlit ocean in the background. When Cedric Gibbons, the renowned art director, brought this blatant snafu to producer Irving Thalberg's attention, Thalberg was unmoved, claiming audiences "...only see about ten percent of what's on the screen anyway, and if they're watching your background instead of my actors, the scene will be

Known as "the necklace on the cutting room floor" this magnificent piece, crafted of sterling silver, cultured pearls, and synthetic emerald stones of exceptionally high quality, appeared in only one scene of 1936's *Camille*. When Greta Garbo later placed a cape around her shoulders, she claimed it dug into her neck and refused to wear it again. The same necklace was commissioned for use in a Jeannette MacDonald film but once again suffered an ill-timed fate. The director was changed in mid-picture, along with a new costume designer. Still housed in the Joseff vault in its velvet presentation case, it remains an elegant example of the glory of film, and a reminder of the power of one of its most mysterious and revered stars...the late Greta Garbo!

"Greta Garbo in the role of Camille . . . was, according to director George Cukor, 'the happy meeting of an actress and a part.'"

(*All-Time Movie Favorites*, p. 54.)

Greta Garbo and Laura Hope Crews, wearing the Joseff necklace shown at right, in a scene from *Camille.*

useless. Whatever you put there they'll believe that's how it is."[1] With that, Gibbons told Thalberg he would be ashamed to ever show his face in France again. Thalberg remained unmoved. He may have underestimated his viewers, however. For:

> ...while cinema audiences contain mercifully few authorities on Elizabethan costumes, they are well able to spot a wristwatch worn by a cutlass-waving pirate...a zip fastener on a kilt, an uplift bra on a Byzantine bosom...all of which have happened and no doubt there is worse to come...We can only console ourselves that the greatest screenwriter of all had clocks striking in ancient Rome....[2]

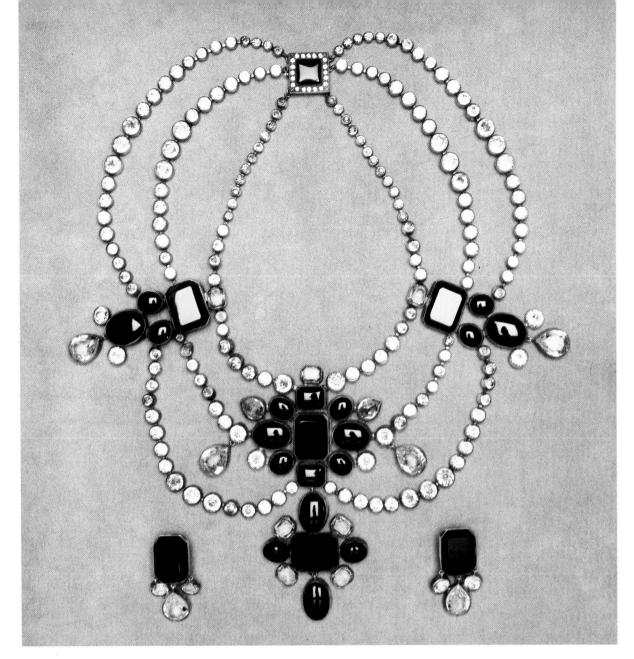

Joseff's design brilliance for *Camille* did not stop with the fabled Camille necklace. This equally magnificent piece was worn by the venerable character actress Laura Hope Crews in the same film. Frank Nugent's *New York Times* review of *Camille* on July 17, 1936, after mentioning the supporting performers, including Laura Hope Crews, wrote "...we have received what we had every right to expect—good, sound supporting performances. That they should have been noted at all, in view of Miss Garbo's brilliant domination of the picture, is high praise indeed."[3]

Well, Joseff, if not an authority on clocks, knew his jewelry and easily recognized an error of monumental proportions, at least to his highly trained eyes, when he viewed *The Affairs of Cellini* in 1934. For there on the screen was the beautiful Constance Bennett, suitably gowned in carefully recreated costumes of sixteenth century Italy, wearing what was obviously twentieth century jewelry, as was an ingenue lady-in-waiting named Lucille Ball. He rushed to tell Plunkett what a disservice this was to costume designers who strove for authenticity and then sullied it by allowing the inclusion of jewelry of questionable genre. Plunkett, not to be outdone, challenged him by replying, "Well, if you're so smart, let's see what you can do."

With friendly, but nonetheless intense fervor, the gauntlet was down and Joseff seized the opportunity. Although he had supplied jewelry and props for a smattering of films prior to this, his career wasn't really launched until that fateful episode with Plunkett. Doors opened that had previously been closed, and Joseff was on his way! Before long he had wrangled tentative designing assignments for several movies—but first he had to ensure that his ideas could be produced to specification. With sketches in hand, he approached a plethora of jewelry manufacturers, all of whom called his designs original and intriguing but impractical and impossible to duplicate. This is the stuff of legends—and the Joseff tale is no exception. For it was then, on the heels of these "rejections," that the legacy of the "Jeweller to the Stars" had its real beginnings.

Determined that his designs *could* be made, there appeared to be only one solution—he would manufacture them himself! To save time and avoid his earlier frustrations, the makeshift workshop was expanded into a full-scale, albeit small, manufacturing operation. Through trial and error, what he initially knew to be true was proven. Jewelry designs considered cost prohibitive or impossible to produce were carefully crafted by Joseff and the "small but mighty" staff he quickly assembled.

Once he received a contract for a specific movie, Joseff's initial effort was aimed at achieving complete authenticity through careful research. He assembled a rare book collection and used their text and illustrations to form the basis of many of his designs. Not only was he successful in reproducing jewels of historical accuracy, but Joseff also cleverly incorporated ideas from his own imagination that correctly captured the look of a given period *and* the mood of the film's creators.

One of Joseff's earlier movie pieces, this spectacular pendant is worn by Heather Angel in the 1935 version of *The Three Musketeers*. The gentleman by her side is Walter Abel.

In some instances, the art director or costume designer furnished the illustrations, at first with little hope that they could be authentically reproduced. Those fears were swiftly allayed when Joseff provided magnificent replicas. If he could have changed one thing during this early period, it would have been the use of more color film, for the care he took in creating brilliantly jeweled reproductions was understandably lost in black and white.

The decision to have total control over every step of the process would prove fortuitous to Joseff's future success, for complete management of his work, from initial designs through the finished product, assured not only the integrity of the jewelry but the speed at which it could be delivered. From the very beginning, he instituted another crucial policy concerning jewelry orders contracted by the studios. In a stroke of forward-thinking business savvy, Joseff decided the pieces would never be sold to the studios—only *rented*. And that is why these "gems of the silver screen" continue to be enjoyed and treasured, with many still appearing time and again in films and on the TV screen. To lease and not sell was a masterful and lucrative business decision, but there was perhaps an added element of a strictly emotional nature, one that many artists also confront...there is frequently great difficulty in relinquishing that over which we have labored so diligently!

In the early 1940s, an article in the *Christian Science Monitor* presented an insightful account of Joseff's dedication to quality and integrity. In part, the interviewer wrote, "One of his boasts is that he has never failed to deliver an order to the studio at the time he promised, though he has had narrow escapes."

The crown worn in 1936 by Katherine Hepburn for her role in *Mary of Scotland* is perfectly paired with a necklace of filigreed balls and its elaborately detailed pendant cross. The costume designer was the gentleman who challenged Joseff to pursue the design of movie jewelry. That he succeeded in convincing Plunkett of his abilities is borne out by Plunkett's letter of praise following this assignment (see p. 73).

The glamour of the movies personified—the fabulous Delores Del Rio! Jewels by Joseff.

A magnificent deco-style bracelet was worn by the always elegant Kay Francis in a 1930's film *Stolen Holiday*. It was written of Ms. Francis that "...she agonized in beautiful clothes over men in dinner jackets in situations that called for a straight face and a stiff chin."[4]

23

The article goes on to recount how an elaborate piece of jewelry for Reginald Denny to wear in *Marie Antoinette* almost didn't arrive before an 8 a.m. Monday deadline. The Joseff staff worked double shifts throughout the weekend, with Joseff giving them pep talks every hour. At dawn on Monday he rushed the finished piece to the studio, only to discover, to his chagrin, that the workmen had neglected to provide little hoops on the back of each jewel so it could be fastened to Denny's outfit. Hoops were obtained from the costume department, and electricians hastily welded them onto the piece in time for the actor to appear in the scene.

A necklace fit for a queen! This one, with matching earrings, adorned the fragile neck of Norma Shearer in *Marie Antoinette*. In a commitment to total authenticity, the making of the film took five years from conception to completion, and was finally released in 1938. It's interesting to note that jewelry played a major role in the pathos of this star-crossed ruler. Through an involved confidence scheme, Marie Antoinette was unfairly accused of spending the Empire's money on a magnificent diamond necklace and other jewelry. This supposed overspending on royal baubles trickled down to blame for most of the country's ills, including the abject poverty then devastating much of France's population. Most historians also agree that she never said, "Let them eat cake," but the accusation remains her probably unjust legacy these many centuries later!

According to John Kobal the film also served a rather interesting and sociological purpose." ...the Shearer vehicle enjoyed a munificence rare even for Hollywood, bestowed on it by Sun King Louis B. Mayer," and was the film that "...set the pattern for Hollywood turning passionately royalist in the mid-1930s."[5]

Norma Shearer *glitters* in this publicity photo for
Marie Antoinette.

Norma Shearer and Tyrone Power in "ring" scene from *Marie Antoinette*. The rings are shown in close-up at the end of the film.

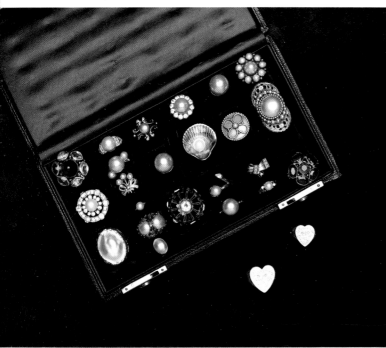

Rings! Rings! Rings! Many seen here were worn in *The Private Lives of Elizabeth and Essex*. The heart rings in front were created for Norma Shearer and Tyrone Power in *Marie Antoinette*. Ms. Shearer later had the design reproduced as wedding rings when she married Marty Arrouge, after the death of Irving Thalberg. They read: "Everything lead me to thee."

In commenting on Shearer's performances in *Romeo and Juliet* (1936), Anita Loos had this advice, "I think the modern American girl has many things to learn from the Juliet of Norma Shearer . . . within the space of twenty minutes Juliet grabs off the best man in Verona, and does it at a time when he is singeing his fingers carrying a torch for another girl. . . . Girls see Norma Shearer as Juliet, and good luck to you."

(*The Hollywood Reporter*, pp. 86-87.)

Opposite page:
Two pieces befitting a queen! The bracelet and amethyst pendant/brooch were worn by Norma Shearer in *Marie Antoinette*. The pendant did double duty when it appeared on Barbara Britton in *The Return of Monte Cristo* (1947), with Louis Hayward.

This staff was carried by Anita Louise in *Anthony Adverse*. The bracelet was worn by Alice Faye in *Lillian Russell*.

This glamourous brooch appeared on the glamourous Jean Harlow (whose name was originally Harlean Carpenter) in the 1936 comedy *Libeled Lady*, also starring Spencer Tracy, Myrna Loy, and William Powell. Although not part of the Powell and Loy *Thin Man* series, could that be Asta in front of this Stutz Bearcat?

Brooch worn by Dietrich nestled in the arms of an Oriental figurine.

The sultry Marlene Dietrich epitomizes the term *temptress* in this publicity shot for *Shanghai Express*. Josef von Sternberg was Marlene Dietrich's mentor, and was responsible for the direction of many of her motion pictures, including *Shanghai Express*. When contracts were negotiated for him, they also were for Marlene. As reported in The Hollywood Reporter, "Professor Henry Higgins never did more for his 'fair lady' than Josef did for "Legs" Dietrich. She received $125,000 a film . . ." A tidy sum for the Depression year of 1932!

Fay Wray wearing necklace at left.

This dynamic "sapphire" necklace and earring parure graced the beautiful Maureen O'Hara in her first film, the unforgettable 1938 version of Victor Hugo's *The Hunchback of Notre Dame*. The earrings were also worn by Fay Wray in a later film.

Six heavy linked chains created quite a statement when worn by Barbara Stanwyck in 1938's *The Mad Miss Manton.*

In a 1954 "Rambling Reporter" article for the Hollywood Reporter, Barbara Stanwyck wrote, "I love to remember the poetic beauty of Robert Taylor and Vivien Leigh in *Waterloo Bridge...*" Since Robert Taylor was the great and abiding love of Stanwyck's life her comment takes on an added poignancy.

(*The Hollywood Reporter*, p. 253.)

In a Caught ... Between Shots column by Joy Zelle for a Hollywood publication of the day, she wrote: "Barbara Stanwyck, celebrating complete recovery from her recent illness, and the completion of her latest RKO Radio picture, "The Mad Miss Manton," was the personification of glamour at the Trocadero with Robert Taylor. Barbara wore bronze hued chiffon—her only jewelry a heavy, six-strand gold chain created by Joseff." In another article on the same subject, Zelle also wrote: "In 'The Mad Miss Manton,' Barbara Stanwyck wore several unique pieces of jewelry. She liked the old-fashioned chatelaines and had Joseff, the designer, create one for her personal collection. Because horses are her hobby ... the chatelaine consists of a medallion of three gold horseheads, with manes flying; from these are suspended tiny gold jockey caps, horseshoes and a gold miniature of her favorite horse, 'The Nut'."

Joseff bracelets are featured in this photo of Rochelle Hudson, a charming 1930's starlet, taken to promote the film *Everybody's Old Man*, starring Irvin S. Cobb.

33

An intricate mass of leaves, berries, and flowers are fashioned into a design masterpiece. The double-strand necklace and bracelet photographed here on Rosemary Lane were also executed by Joseff for Barbara Stanwyck to wear in 1938's *Always Goodbye*, a remake of 1934's *Gallant Lady*, another heart-wrenching tale of mother love in the genre of *Stella Dallas*.

34

This faux ruby/diamond necklace was worn by eighteen-year-old starlet Olympe Bradna in 1938's *Say It in French*, with Ray Milland.

The caption accompanying this promotional photo of Olympe Bradna, shown here wearing the Joseff choker at left read in part, "Olympe Bradna . . . upon reaching her 18th birthday, is now privileged to accept the romantic advances from the young blades of Hollywood." Olympe's parents had adhered to the rule that she have no romantic attachment until she reached that magic age!

Early turban drawing.

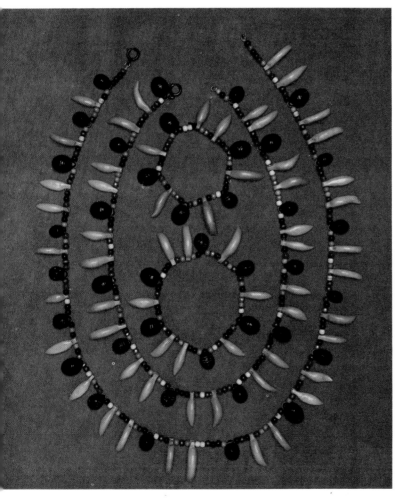

This double "tooth" necklace with matching bracelet gave a jungle ambiance to opera star Lily Pons' appearance in the aptly titled *Hitting a New High* (1937), with Jack Oakie and Lucille Ball.

Roland Young in elaborate, bejewelled garb for his role in the 1937 film *Ali Baba Goes to Town*, also starring comedian Eddie Cantor and Tony Martin— *and* Louise Hovick, who later changed her name to Gypsy Rose Lee!

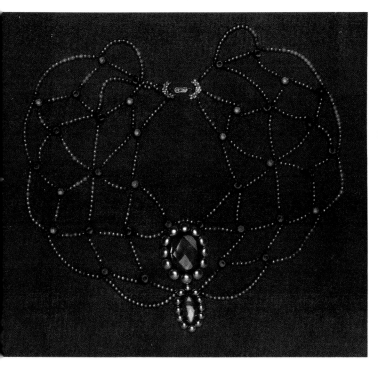

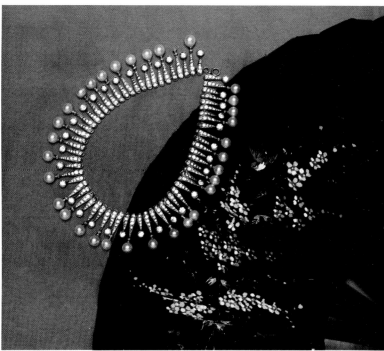

Ilona Massey could only have been stunningly beautiful in this gossamer pearl and aquamarine bib for the 1947 film *Northwest Outpost*.

First appearing on Lana Turner in *Marriage is a Private Affair* (1944), this diamond and pearl necklace was later worn by the ethereal Ingrid Bergman in 1948's *Arch of Triumph*.

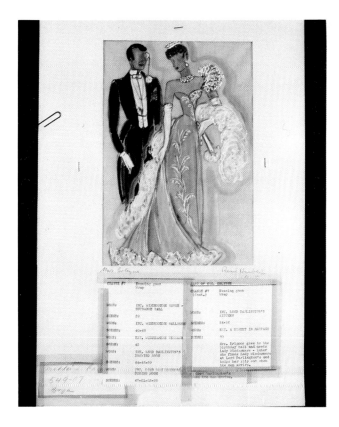

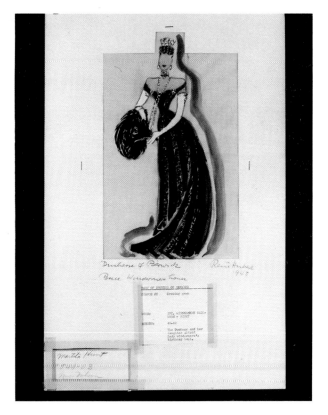

Rene Hubert's 1949 costume design drawings from *Lady Windemere's Fan*, later changed to simply *The Fan*, show portions of script and concept of jewelry later

designed and executed by Joseff. The film starred Madeleine Carroll and George Sanders.

Joseff designed this crown in 1935 to be worn by Helen Gahagan (Mrs. Melvyn Douglas) in *She*, adapted from H. Ryder Haggard's tale of a queen who is seeking the reincarnation of her dead lover and an expedition in quest of the Flame of Eternal Life. The score was by Max Steiner, whose music later added to the powerful impact of *Gone with the Wind*.

This exquisite crown remains as impressive today as it was when worn by Ronald Coleman in 1937's *The Prisoner of Zenda*.

One of Joseff's most difficult assignments occurred early in his career when he was given ten days to reproduce a Cellini cup for an RKO film *The Riddle of the Dangling Pearl*. Since the original cup was on display at the Metropolitan Museum in New York City, he hastily flew to New York, photographed the cup from all angles, and hastily returned by air to California. Arriving late on Saturday evening, he proceeded to make the design drawings for the original and its double—yes, even some movie jewelry required a double—located a foundry that was open on Sunday, and had the Cellini reproductions in RKO's hands bright and early Monday morning. Such was the dedication of Eugene Joseff—and it never wavered!

In the midst of this ever-changing scenario, James Joseff also found his niche, joining his brother in the jewelry business, as a studio representative and Joseff's right-hand man. Later, taking advantage of the California land and property boom that flourished for decades, he turned his selling skills to real estate. The glitter of Hollywood remained with James Joseff, however—first in his association with his brother and then in his marriage to Leah Rhodes, the renowned designer who won an Academy Award in 1945 for the costuming of *Saratoga Trunk* starring Ingrid Bergman and Gary Cooper—with jewelry by none other than her brother-in-law Eugene Joseff!

As Joseff's movie assignments grew so did his reputation. The industry had never seen anything to match it and, in short order, all the major studios recognized the multi-faceted talents of this gentleman from Chicago. Suddenly *they* needed *him* as much as *he* needed them! It was a mutually beneficial arrangement.

It was during these early associations with the film industry that Eugene Joseff's marketing skills once again surfaced, this time with regard to his name. Since his last one could also have been his first, he adopted the single name of Joseff. From that time on, friends, family and business associates rarely referred to him in any other way. In fact, few people even knew or questioned what his first name might be. Being simply Joseff was eminently suited to his personality and demeanor, adding an air of mystery and professionalism. Just as one is said to be "born to the purple," so was Eugene Joseff born to be only Joseff! The sole additions to this single moniker were used in advertising and promotional material, when he was referred to as "Joseff of Hollywood" and "Joseff: Jeweller to the Stars."

By 1938, Joseff's business was booming. His credits included the vast majority of movies produced during that time. There was one major problem, however. Mountains of paperwork engulfed his office. Bills weren't presented on time, or by any particular system. He desperately needed an assistant.

Enter Joan Castle...

Opposite page:
This intricate golden scepter is from *The Prisoner of Zenda*. The jeweled treasure chest made a magnificent prop for *Gigi* in 1958.

Scene III
Enter Joan Castle

Joan Castle was born in rural Alberta, Canada, but grew up in Oregon. Blessed with high intelligence and innate common sense, she excelled in her college classes, especially those related to business. Joseff, on the other hand, followed the path of many artistic geniuses. Designing and initiating ideas were his forte. The details of running a business were not.

And thus, the fates began moving these two very different, and yet very alike individuals in a direction that would culminate in a many-faceted partnership. That JC (as her family, associates, and friends still call her) decided to leave Oregon at the height of the Depression and seek her education—and hopefully, fortune—in the vastly different environment of California was the first magnetic step. That she was drawn to UCLA was the second, and that after graduation she decided to enroll in Sawyer Business School so she could earn money to return to UCLA for an advanced degree was the third. Joseff's desperate call to Sawyer to send their best and brightest student to help organize his office was the fourth. And the fact that they immediately chose Joan was the final force that drew them together!

It didn't take Joan Castle long to conclude that the sophisticated, debonair Joseff took exceptional pride in his research, designs, and finished product. It was evident, however, that these were understandably consuming all of his time, and the paperwork and general business details that had to be attended to in any operation had created loose ends that were in danger of unraveling.

The Depression caused severe financial difficulties for some in the movie industry, especially during the grim, early years, but for Joseff the problems were minimal. The public flocked to the movies, especially during the latter half of the 1930s. Now more than ever they depended on those few stolen hours in the theatre as an inexpensive and entertaining form of escapism in an unsettled world, and movie czars continued to "churn" out film after film at mind-boggling speed. Hollywood was entering its heyday.

When Joan reminisces about those first weeks with Joseff, she's quick to say that it was a case of love at first sight. "But I couldn't let him know it. The orders were pouring in. All the studios wanted his services. In fact, we could barely keep up, sometimes working through the night to make promised deliveries first thing in the morning." JC managed to get the office upheaval under control and convinced Joseff that drastic changes had to be made if he wanted to continue.

Before long Joan was firmly entrenched in the Joseff operation and became an irreplaceable asset. Since their foundries could easily be converted to defense work, the start of World War II opened new vistas for many jewelry manufacturers. Soon the production of Joseff jewelry shared equal billing with small airplane parts! Now there were government contracts to be dealt with, as well as the standard movie ones. Although a seemingly strange manufacturing combination, this new arm of the business opened a door that would prove beneficial for years to come. Joan's role became critical to what was now a booming jewelry and war effort business. And Joan Castle did one more very crucial thing. She secretly captured Joseff's heart. The team, at least in their private thoughts, was no longer a business one!

The ensuing romance had a fairy tale quality befitting the unlikely beginnings of the princely Joseff and his Canadian princess. Bringing Eugene Joseff and Joan Castle together, sometimes for twelve and eighteen hour days—or even longer when plagued by a seemingly impossible deadline—with both striving for perfection in something they jointly loved, created the bond that formed a solid foundation for their marriage in 1942.

The circumstances of the meeting and courtship of Joseff and JC bear an uncanny resemblance to the story line of many movies of the era in which Joseff jewelry appeared. Screen heroines of the Rosalind Russell, Katherine Hepburn, or Barbara Stanwyck genre would have fit the roll to a "T." Here was a recent coed, newly graduated from college, whose first opportunity is to assist an attractive, unmarried man, somewhat older than she, who is involved in an outwardly glamorous occupation among glamourous people—movies stars! This young woman falls in love with him on sight—and truth be known, he probably does the same.

But they can't confess their feelings until much later in the relationship, so they work side by side, their attraction never openly expressed. The heroine turns out to be remarkably intelligent and astute. The hero needs her, first professionally and later personally. The couple, usually under "slapstick" circumstances, finally confess their love and head for the altar. True love is once again triumphant, the audience applauds, and everyone leaves the theatre happy! Screenwriters of the day had worked and reworked this script to a fare-thee-well. Which proves once again that most so-called fiction is indeed no stranger to fact.

True to the aforementioned "slapstick" circumstances, Joseff created a scenario that was charming, witty, and deceptively romantic. In November, 1942, Joan singlehandedly completed a particularly difficult promotional assignment for which Joseff was enormously grateful. As a special "thank you," Joseff told her he needed to measure her right ring finger. He'd decided to make a ring for Joan, using a particularly beautiful aquamarine surrounded by rubies. But that wasn't all. Joseff wanted to add yet another token of appreciation, offering to take JC any place her heart desired—providing they could reach their destination within 24 hours! Joan's choice was a practical one. Never having been there, she opted for the excitement of Las Vegas and, with two other couples in tow, they set off for a weekend celebration.

A pensive foo dog with Oriental lady adds a background of intrigue to this intricately detailed bracelet with deep green carved center stone, worn by Ona Munson (above) in 1941's *Shanghai Gesture*. Directed by Josef von Sternberg, the film starred Gene Tierney, Walter Houston and Victor Mature. Mothers have played important and nurturing roles in countless films. However, in *Shanghai Gesture* the mold was broken when Madame Gin Sling shoots her own daughter!

43

A massive "emerald" and rhinestone spray and bracelet worn by Rosemary Lane (one of the three beautiful Lane sisters) in *The Oklahoma Kid* (1939), also starring James Cagney, Humphrey Bogart, and Ward Bond.

This frog on a lily pad was also worn by Rosemary Lane, for *Oklahoma Kid*.

This sparkling crystal necklace and bracelet were originally worn by Fay Wray in an early film. The bracelet was later worn by Rosemary Lane in *Oklahoma Kid*.

This "emerald" and pearl necklace and "climb the arm" bracelet added to Hedy Lamarr's mysterious aura in 1938's *Algiers,* (shown in studio shot on the arm of Joan Leslie). The film also starred the debonair Charles Boyer as Pepe LeMoko. Ten years later, it was remade as a musical and named *Casbah.*

Opposite:
This gigantic brooch, modeled by a stunningly demure Jane Wyman, is a one-of-a-kind piece that cannot be duplicated. Joan Joseff still wears it—to many oohs and aahs!

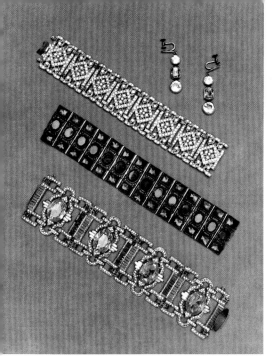

Three bracelets and faux diamond and emerald earrings. All were worn by Angela Lansbury in *The Harvey Girls* (1946), starring Judy Garland and featuring the Oscar-winning song, "Atchison, Topeka, and Santa Fe" by Johnny Mercer.

Angela Lansbury relaxing between scenes on the set of *The Harvey Girls* with Preston Foster and Kenny Baker.

48

This Joseff brooch and bracelet are a knockout! From the 1948 Universal film *Casbah*, this is the scene where Pepe (Tony Martin) tells Gaby (Marta Toren) that he has been exiled to the casbah in order to avoid the French police. The movie also starred Yvonne de Carlo and Peter Lorre.

The swirling beauty on right was straight from the *Casbah* and worn by Marta Toren. Evelyn Keyes wore the one on the left in *The Killer That Stalked New York*.

Janet Leigh, mother of Jamie Lee Curtis, wears
Joseff necklace for her role as Mrs. Richard Rodgers
in *Words and Music* (1948).

A magnificent butterfly also designed for Janet
Leigh in 1948's *Words and Music*, a musical extrav-
aganza about the song-writing team of Richard
Rodgers and Lorenz Hart, with an all-star cast
including Mickey Rooney, June Allyson, Judy
Garland, Gene Kelly, Perry Como, and Cyd Charisse.

50

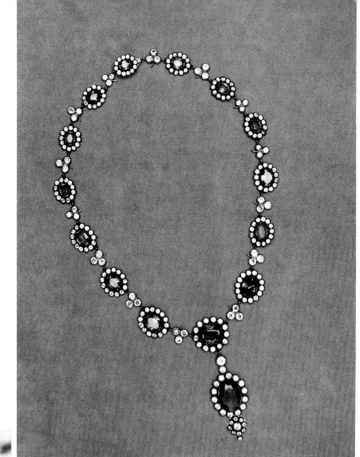

Although not chronologically, this amethyst and diamond beauty adorned the necks of three generations. From a youthful Deanna Durbin in the movie version of the Broadway hit *Up in Central Park* (1948), to Bette Davis in *The Story of a Divorce* (1950), to the elderly Dame May Whitty in *This Time for Keeps* (1947).

Dame May Whitty and Jimmy Durante in a scene from *This Time for Keeps*, 1947. Whitty was a mainstay in films of the era—a delightful character actress who played drama and comedy with equal ease.

Jointed sections of pearls and rhinestones designed in the Joseff tradition for Gloria Grahame in *Merton of the Movies* (1947).

The beauty of topaz and Joseff's special antiquing process combine in this brooch designed for Anna Sten in *Let's Live a Little* (1948).

These elegant diamond and sapphire pieces are worthy of a chauffeured limousine. They were worn by Lucille Ball in *Annabel Takes a Tour* (1938).

Lucille Ball was never lovelier than in this 1941 publicity photo for *Look Who's Laughing*. The Joseff ball and tassel necklace and bracelet complete this stunning photograph.

A resplendent Akim Tamiroff poses in full regalia for 1939's *The Magnificent Fraud*. Apparently the studio needed a poster advertising Tamiroff as an impersonator of King Henry VIII and planned to use an actual portrait of the *real* king. Tamiroff would have none of it, and spent five hours perfecting and donning this elaborate makeup and costuming in order that the still photo above could be taken.

This photo shows Tamiroff again—this time as Napoleon, one of five roles he assumes in *The Magnificent Fraud*. Although he had long wanted to play Napoleon, he appears as "the little corporal" in only one brief appearance.

This turban brooch, companion piece to the necklaces, was worn by Virginia Bruce in *There Goes My Heart*.

This charm necklace was designed for Heather Thatcher to wear in 1938's *Fools for Scandal*, directed by Mervyn LeRoy and starring Carole Lombard. It's photographed here on starlet Evelyn Knapp.

Designed for the personal wardrobe of Kay Francis, a duplicate was worn by Mary Astor in *Woman Against Woman*, and is modeled here by a youthful Rita Hayworth.

Deanna Durbin looks wonderfully elegant, yet demure, in this publicity shot for *Up in Central Park*, wearing necklace pictured on page 49.

Necklace worn by Loretta Young in *Bedtime Story*, a 1941 comedy also starring Frederic March.

A Joseff necklace adds to the ethereal quality of Loretta Young in this scene from 1939's *Wife, Husband, and Friend.*

Ona Munson wore this magnificent topaz necklace in *Shanghai Gesture* (1941). It was later worn by many screen beauties, including Alice Faye in *That Night in Rio* (1941), Tallulah Bankhead in *Royal Scandal* (1945), and Linda Darnell in *Forever Amber* (1947) and is probably Joseff's most "often used" piece.

Tallulah Bankhead wearing *the* necklace in *A Royal Scandal*. In addition to its appearances in films, the necklace also appeared in the TV series *The New Mission Impossible* and was displayed in Australia as "The Most Fabulous Necklace in the World."

Arriving too early to check into their hotel, the partygoers strolled to a nearby cafe for a leisurely drink. Joan recalls sipping a ginger ale while everyone else relaxed with something more festive. And then, in the midst of their happy conversation and laughter, Joseff playfully pulled a tiny box from his pocket and presented it to Joan. Inside was another ring, also a Joseff original, in an openwork design of gold leaves with twinkling diamonds (she later learned that this represented the four seasons and signified eternal love). Since it wasn't the typical diamond setting one would associate with an engagement ring, Joan reasoned that it was simply another very generous gift—a bonus, like the aquamarine and the jaunt to Las Vegas. But then Joseff said, rather offhandedly, "Since you've managed my business affairs so beautifully, how would you like to do the same for my personal life?" It was a bona fide proposal of marriage! Her female companions were ecstatic—the gentlemen somewhat more reserved, but everyone was talking at once, and everyone was telling her, "Marry him! Marry him!"

Almost before a magician could intone "abracadabra," the newly-assembled wedding party was inside the courthouse, and Joan and Joseff had applied for, and quickly received, a marriage license. This progressed so rapidly, in fact, that the participants didn't even venture out of the building to search for a suitable place to tie the knot! The female clerk urged them to have the "in-house" Justice of the Peace perform the ceremony, declaring that he looked "just like Clark Gable." Well the clerk was either nearsighted or blindly in love with the Justice herself, for he bore no resemblance to Gable or any other Hollywood heartthrob. Not that it mattered. At that moment, the gentleman by Joan's side was Clark Gable and all of Hollywood's leading men rolled into one!

In the tradition of most Hollywood scripts of like genre, this tale had to hit a snag or two, and true to form it did! For when the moment came for Joseff to slide the ring on Joan's finger, it wouldn't budge past her second knuckle. Most hands are not identical in size, and Joan's were no exception. Her left ring finger was larger than the right one he'd measured for the aquamarine. Determined that nothing was going to interfere with making this a ceremony to be remembered— and that the ring would go on her left hand, where it belonged—JC pushed with all her might and forced it over the offending knuckle. There was no way this little lady was going to marry Eugene Joseff without that ring securely on her finger when the judge declared, "I now pronounce you man and wife." Snag one successfully resolved! Snag two followed swiftly. In the middle of the night JC's finger had swollen so painfully that a jeweler had to be routed out of bed to cut the ring off!

Working together as husband and wife added a new dimension to the "fairy tale" of Joseff and JC—again, bearing an uncanny resemblance to those famous on-screen couples like Loy and Powell and Tracy and Hepburn. They too were the ultimate in "teamsmanship," and an unbeatable one at that.

When she reminisces about her wedding day, Joan still laughingly recalls the chatter of her friends as they urged her to marry Joseff. Did they think for a moment that she wouldn't? Prince Charming had long ago captured the heart of fair maiden!

These hair combs were worn by Ann Blyth in *Mr. Peabody and the Mermaid* (1948) as she cavorted with "creatures of the deep."

Janis Carter and Lloyd Corrigan in a scene from *The Fighting Guardsman*, 1945. The topaz set is pictured at right.

Another bib of monumental proportions. This one worn by Maria Montez in *Pirates of Monterey* (1947).

This "Neptunian" crown sat regally on the head of sultry Maria Montez in *Siren of Atlantis* (1948). As Jesse Lasky, Jr. wrote so descriptively of Ms. Montez, "She oozed patent, blatant allure. She was a panther of pleasure...she glided into a room, hips undulating, eyes like dark cauldrons in which the virtue of a saint could be dissolved."[1]

Virginia Bruce wearing massive acrylic headdresss for her role in *The Great Ziegfeld* (1936).

Barbara Britton as she appeared in *The Return of Monte Cristo* (1946)

The Great Ziegfeld won an Oscar for "best picture of 1936 "and garnered a "best actress" award for Luis Rainer. Highlight of film was when Virginia Bruce, wearing headpiece above left, descended a huge staircase while Dennis Morgan stood at the bottom singing "A Pretty Girl is Like a Melody."

This necklace was created for Barbara Bates to wear in the 1949 film *Quicksand*, also starring Mickey Rooney.

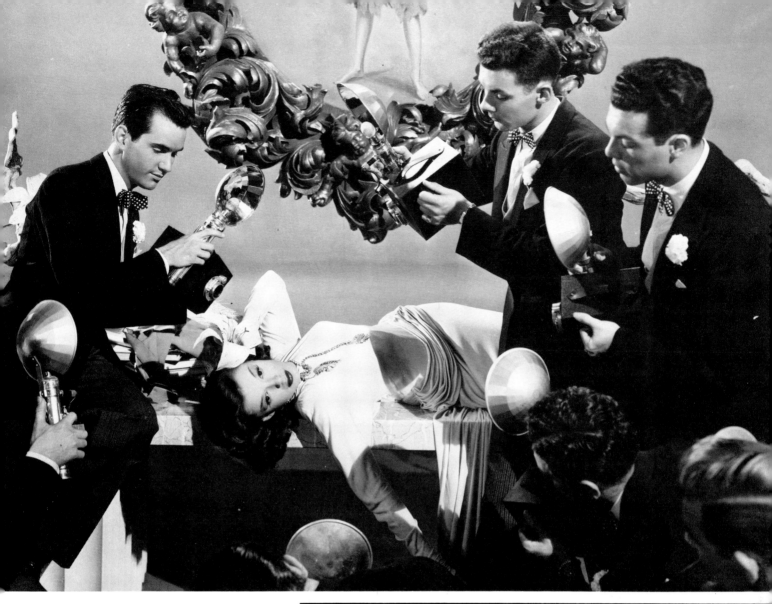

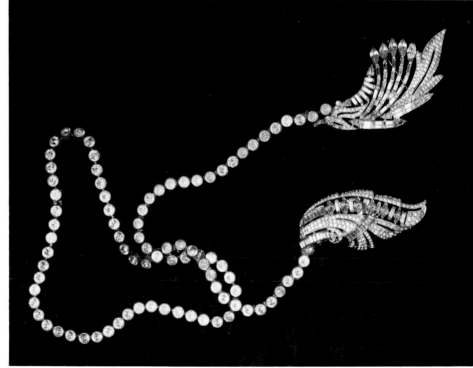

An interesting lariat design with a diamond-look, worn by Judy Garland in *Ziegfeld Follies*, directed by her future husband, Vincent Minnelli. *Follies* had an all-star cast, including William Powell, Lucille Ball, Lena Horne, Gene Kelly, Fred Astaire, and countless others.

Stunning in design and execution, these personalized
pieces consisting of a necklace, brooches and earrings
incorporate the initial of Lord Nelson, and were
worn by his lover Lady Hamilton in *That Hamilton
Woman* starring Lawrence Olivier and Vivian Leigh.
This film, titled simply *Lady Hamilton* in Britain, is said
to have been, along with *The Sea Hawk*, Churchill's
favorite historical film. Produced by Alexander Korda
the costumes were by Rene Hubert.

Scene IV
Movies—The Golden Years

Although the 1970s and 1980s were socioeconomically ripe for a *revolution*, most advocates of today's women's liberation movement acknowledge that this is by no means a new concept. Instead, its early stirrings are quite appropriately associated with the serious causes of suffragettes and birth control advocates in the early years of the twentieth century, as well as the more frivolous but nonetheless feminist statements to be found in the bobbed hair, short skirts, jazz and Charlestons of the 1920s. Not aware of the eventual magnitude of their on-screen roles, there were other pioneers, however, whose place in the movement was a far-reaching one. For even a casual look at the movies of the 1930s and 1940s—and to a considerably lesser extent the 1950s—shows a trend that now appears astonishingly "before its time" in terms of our present view of the so-called "modern woman." Whether by design or happenstance, these movies and their sometimes subtle-sometimes overt messages reached more women in a shorter period of time than the leaders of nationwide suffragette parades or writers of newspaper headlines and articles could ever have hoped for.

During this period, Rosalind Russell typified the earnest woman with a mind of her own in film after film, like 1940's *Hired Wife*, co-starring Brian Aherne, and *His Girl Friday* with Cary Grant. Katherine Hepburn was certainly no shrinking violet in *The Philadelphia Story*, or in her strong-willed, battle-of-wits roles in 1942's *Woman of the Year* and 1949's *Adam's Rib*, both of which pitted her against—and yet always *with* —her equally strong co-star, Spencer Tracy (a masterful nuance of acting skill that only two great talents could make believable).

Whether playing a domineering yet vulnerable queen in 1939's *The Private Lives of Elizabeth and Essex* or a sloe-eyed siren in 1938's *Jezebel*, Bette Davis showed amazing versatility. Barbara Stanwyck was more than a match for the likes of Gary Cooper and Fred MacMurray, and Joan Crawford's image in roles that ran the gamut from conniving temptress to demanding female executive, combined sensuality with hard-driving ambition in an imperious way that has rarely been equaled.

In the *Thin Man* series, Myrna Loy's input was just as vital to solving the crime as William Powell's and, regardless of her sometimes scatter-brained mannerisms and seemingly outward dependency, she never took a "back seat" to her male counterpart. This tendency was also evident in the work of other actresses of the day, including Claudette Colbert, Jean Arthur, Irene Dunne, Jean Harlow and Carole Lombard, all of whom more often than not had an extra dollop of fun with their characters, adding a comedic touch that was not only appealing but deliciously disarming. More assertive on-screen women were in the majority, although not always portrayed in the most flattering light, as is clearly evident in 1939's *The Women*. However, through it all these beauties maintained an aura of femininity and glamour. Even when the script called for the female lead to generate a hard exterior, there was frequently an underlying soft, magnetic quality that belied what one initially expected of the character they portrayed.

When cast as the "other woman" in a triangle between a fresh-faced, starry-eyed innocent and the handsome hero, these leading ladies, and more frequently the always vital supporting actresses, radiated this same inescapable charm, coupled with a gumption that was intriguingly admirable. They may have *lost* the leading man but somehow we knew they'd forge ahead, temporarily disappointed perhaps, but sensing instinctively that something "better" was just around the corner!

These roles represented a point of view quite different from the one society had led mature women and blossoming young girls to expect, and many strove to emulate their example, all the while feeling somewhat disloyal for having secretly hoped that the pre-ordained plot of "nice girl meets nice boy and lives happily ever after" would be surprisingly overturned. As a group, these stars and their counterparts—the "never get their man" starlets and second leads—had created a whole new approach to the feminine mystique.

The stage may not have been totally set for a full-scale upheaval in the scenario of woman's exact rung on society's ladder, but the props were definitely in place, just waiting for the curtain to go up. Indeed, the royal ladies in those wonderful movies of the 1930s and 1940s left a legacy of permanent blossoms, for the seeds had been carefully, if somewhat inadvertently, nurtured during their reign.

Viewed by today's standards and circumstances, many of these films may seem outdated, even amusing. The preface to *Kitty Foyle*, the 1940 film of a 1930's "working girl" for which Ginger Rogers won an Oscar in the title role, is an outstanding example. In its preface, brief vignettes are shown depicting the progression of women's rights from the turn of the century to the time of Kitty's entry into the ranks of a secretary trying to "make it" in New York. The vignettes ended with suffragettes emerging triumphant when females were finally granted the right to vote. And then we read on the screen, "...and so the battle was won and women got their equal rights." Not quite! But female viewers of 1940 most likely agreed, and gave themselves a hearty pat on the back. When considering the treatment of a myriad of social and moral issues on the screen, it must be remembered that "...the film-makers of the thirties and forties lived in a different world from our own; they accepted different premises and applied different standards, which were not necessarily wrong because they now seem dated and reactionary."[1] The same standards should apply when judging the audiences of the day.

Eugene Joseff forged his own imprint in these stirrings of sociological upheaval. A master at capturing not only the essence of the past but the trends of the present, his jewelry reflected this dynamic on-screen metamorphosis. In many of his movie creations, bolder, more tailored designs are evident, and these same concepts eventually carried over to the Joseff retail pieces. For film, it was a

Left: Ornate Suez necklace adapted by Joseff from pieces designed by Royer, Twentieth Century-Fox Studio stylist, for Loretta Young to wear in the picture *Suez*. Photographed on Kay Sutton.

A tiara and hair comb designed for Loretta Young to wear in *Suez*. The comb was originally studded with genuine rubies, which were later replaced with emeralds for use in another film.

Ten strands of pearls are draped around a center section featuring a fabulous brooch with cascading stones. Worn by Bette Davis in *The Private Lives of Elizabeth and Essex*, it also appeared on the manly chest of Tyrone Power in *The Rains Came* (1939).

These powerful pieces also added much to the handsome countenance of Tyrone Power in *The Rains Came*, co-starring Myrna Loy. The dagger was used many times over the ensuing years, and the belt was worn again in 1951 by Anthony Dexter in his portrayal of Valentino.

case of scriptwriter, director, and actors, as well as costume and jewelry designer, working together in perfect sync. And it happened with precision time after time. Joseff may have played a major, albeit "behind the scenes," role, but the presentation was as close to perfection as one could conceivably expect. The costume designers were ecstatic.

From Royer at Twentieth Century Fox, December, 1938:

...The execution of the design far exceeded my expectations. In fact, I had no idea you could give it that unusual touch which the average jeweler lacks. Everyone here has greatly admired it, not only for its intricate workmanship, but for its practicality and beauty....More and more we motion picture designers realize that...the costume is no more important than the accessories....

From Walter Plunkett at Selznick International Pictures, January 1939:

"The things you did for me on *Mary of Scotland* and all the others were so beautifully done that of course you know that you will be the only one I will consider to carry out my designs."

And, in 1938, from the designer at Columbia Pictures:

"It will be simple to keep you advised on all new ideas and, whenever it is possible, to use some of your latest pieces....It may be to our mutual advantage to design a gown to accent the jewelry."

As the 1950s made their entrance, however, the trend was for female stars to be relegated to more passive, less controversial roles. There were, of course, exceptions, like Rosalind Russell's striking performance as a college dean in 1950's *A Woman of Distinction*, in which she wore a dramatic Joseff necklace that had, in fact, first appeared on Kay Francis in the Deanna Durbin film *It's a Date* ten years earlier (see p. 171). The fact that the basic material was of wood added to its assertiveness, yet the large but restrained stones gave the piece and its wearer a decidedly feminine quality.

After the uncertainties and loneliness of the war years, postwar conditions seemed to encourage, even demand, a reversion to the safe haven of family and the comfort of the "tried and true." As women relaxed into the role of wife, mother and helpmate in the cocoon of suburbia that sprang into being with a housing "boom" of unprecedented proportions, it was only logical that movies would generally follow suit by presenting heroines more in keeping with the mood of the times.

The 1950s marked the end of an era for a bevy of unique female stars. It is highly unlikely, in fact virtually impossible, that the movie decades that preceded it could ever again be duplicated. "As this century comes to a close, the great female stars are in short supply, especially when compared to the pre-1950s...they had star power, staying power undimmed by age and the face of fashion."[2]

We shall never see their like again, for the circumstances and environment that created them has long vanished. If not already destroyed by time and neglect, the performances of these dazzling damsels can only be enjoyed on the far less intimate television screen and in often grainy rental videos...or simply in the fond and poignant memories of those who were fortunate enough to have admired them on the "big" screens of that long ago time and place!

The Private Lives of Elizabeth and Essex, even though in black and white, showcased Joseff's creations to excellent advantage, as seen in this gigantic amber and pearl brooch, worn by Bette Davis.

The 1939 production of *The Private Lives of Elizabeth and Essex* involved 13 months of research and cost $1,500,000—including the highest costume budget in Warner Bros.' 30-year history.

One of Joseff's many crowns flanks a necklace and bracelet worn by Bette Davis in *The Private Lives of Elizabeth and Essex*. The necklace later switched gender when it appeared around Tyrone Power's neck in *The Rains Came,* and also, with slight variation, on Anthony Quinn's head in Sinbad the Sailor (p. 101).

This elegant nine-strand bib of pearls, accented by gold filigree sections studded with "rubies" added a powerful air of regality to the austere presence of Bette Davis in *The Private Lives of Elizabeth and Essex* (1939), as did her resplendent array of jewelry in the publicity shot at left.

Alice Faye in her role as *Lillian Russell* (1940) with co-star Don Ameche. A newspaper article of the day reported that . . . "Lillian Russell's great love of jewelry will be perpetuated in the Twentieth Century Fox production . . . the picture is one of the most lavish as to costumes and jewelry made in many seasons. Travis Banton designed the costumes and collaborated with Joseff of Hollywood in the designing of the jewelry . . ." One tiara of three "fountains of diamonds" was taken from an 1860 design. The paper went on to report that even Ms. Russell's famous diamond dog collar was reproduced, as well as an enormous pin that simulated three dragonflies in rubies and diamonds.

(Shown on page 78.)

Two "diamond and emerald" brooches and a gold and emerald cuff bracelet, all worn by Alice Faye in *Lillian Russell.*

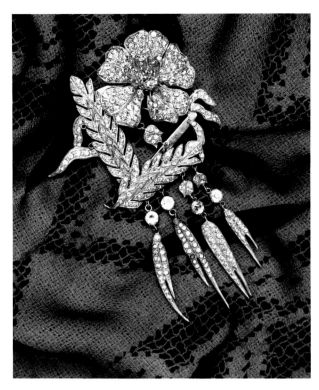

Alice Faye must have looked "splendiferous" in this whopper of a brooch, designed for *Lillian Russell*.

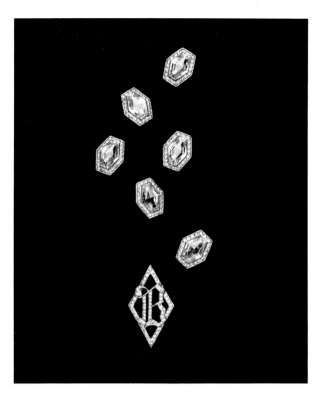

Joseff jewelry wasn't limited to glamorous female stars. The portly Edward Arnold wore this brooch and cuff links set in *Diamond Jim* (1935), a role he repeated in 1940's *Lillian Russell*, with its all-star cast, including Alice Faye, Don Ameche, and Henry Fonda.

This intricate creation is both delicate and bold! It's called a *stomacher* and graced the hour-glass figure of Alice Faye in *Lillian Russell*.

78

As described in press material for *My Wild Irish Rose*, "This wonderful evening dress is made of pure gold thread lame fabric, entirely covered with black maline which is heavily embroidered with black spangles and black jet drops. The embroidery is in authentic period motifs and fringes of black bead and sequin ball tassels drop from the pattern. A trifle stupendous, but very Lillian Russell." And let's not overlook the jewelry by Joseff, which certainly added to the elaborate costuming.

Lillian Russell was a popular subject for film in the 1930s and 1940s. In 1947's *My Wild Irish Rose* she was portrayed by Andrea King, who wore this beautiful bracelet and elaborate earrings. This movie, however, centered on the life of Chauncey Olcott, and also starred Dennis Morgan and Arlene Dahl.

Rhinestones are not *just* rhinestones, as these beautiful bracelets, necklaces, and brooches in varying designs, can attest. Time and again they have all graced the wrists, necks, and bosoms of movie and television stars!

This dress, worn by Greer Garson in *Mrs. Miniver* was acquired by Joan Joseff at auction. The necklace was used in several different films.

Baubles, bangles and beads! These are the bangles—all worn by Marlene Dietrich in *Kismet* (1943) co-starring Ronald Coleman.

Another grouping of much-used movie pieces. The center one was worn by Ida Lupino in 1944's *Hollywood Canteen*, a take-off on the haven for servicemen that actually existed in "Tinseltown" during World War II, and was founded by Bette Davis and John Garfield. The one at right is shown above in a Universal Studios publicity photo that captures the *look* associated with this era.

Double-strand necklace and bracelet designed by Royer, Twentieth Century-Fox studio stylist, and adapted by Joseff for Barbara Stanwyck to wear in the picture *Always Goodbye*. Photographed on Rosemary Lane.

In a 1954 article for The Hollywood Reporter, Barbara Stanwyck wrote, "I lack the words to express the 1st but not the least of my memories—no words are worthy of the unforgettable, the incomparable—Hell! I need only one word anyway. Here it is—Garbo!" (*The Hollywood Reporter*, p. 67)

Gail Patrick, wearing sunburst Leo clips for her role in 1941's *Suspicion*, starring Cary Grant and Joan Fontaine.

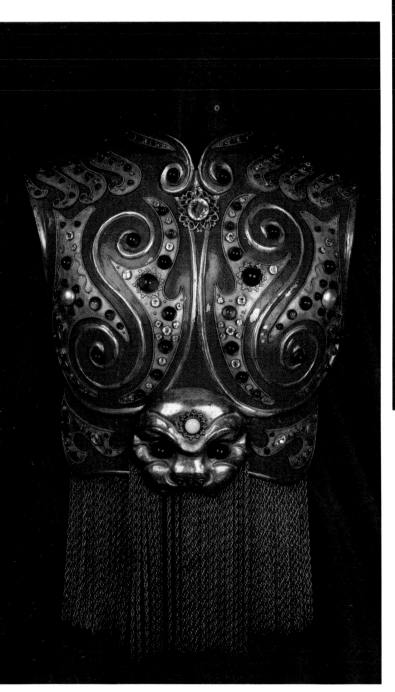

This majestic hat of muted colors captures the dark undertones of 1942's *The Jungle Book*, starring Sabu as a boy raised by wolves. (Remade by Disney in 1967)

Opposite page top:
The three thieves in *The Jungle Book* display the wonderful jeweled armour created by Joseff.

Opposite page bottom:
A masterpiece! From Alexander Korda's *The Jungle Book* (1942) starring Sabu, a belt and gauntlet combining power and raw beauty. The gauntlet (a jeweled weapon worn on the arm) was also a part of Victor Mature's scanty wardrobe in *Samson and Delilah* six years later.

Breathtakingly powerful, this breastplate is one of three worn by the thieves in *The Jungle Book* and is accented by mythical gold head and chain mail, a companion piece to the belt (shown opposite).

Although contracted for numerous films featuring different stars, these aquamarine pieces complement each other. The smaller one at top was worn by the petite Janet Gaynor, the round one was worn by Bette Davis in *The Sisters*, and later by Susan Hayward in *The Saxon Charm*.

This stunning double rhinestone bow and dual chokers were also worn by Marily Maxwell in 1948's *Summer Holiday*.

Platinum blonde Marilyn Maxwell appears here in her first role as a screen siren for MGM's *Summer Holiday* (1947), a musical adaptation of Eugene O'Neill's *Ah, Wilderness*. Her jewels by Joseff include a gem-studded cigarette holder.

The gifted British actress Gladys Cooper in a scene from 1944's *Mrs. Parkington* starring Greer Garson and Walter Pidgton. Cooper had previously won an Academy Award for her 1943 performance in *The Song of Bernadette*.

Gladys Cooper, again, this time in period costume with Lana Turner and Edmund Gwenn in a scene from *Green Dolphin Street*, the 1946 film about early days in New Zealand and the Channel Islands. Also starring were Van Heflin and Donna Reed. Here Cooper wears onyx brooch, minus the center drop, which was added later.

"Emeralds and pearls." A beautiful combination for Katina Paxinou to wear in *Mourning Becomes Electra,* the 1947 film starring Rosalind Russell.

HOLLYWOOD'S LAST GREAT MOVIE LEGENDS

THE MOVIES WE LOVED

Those eyes, that mouth: Bette starred with Paul Muni, John Garfield & Brian Aherne in *Juarez* (1939).

◄ The daring 1934 role that started critics raving: Millie the waitress in *Of Human Bondage*.

▼ Bette was a spoiled socialite and Ronald Reagan was her dapper buddy in *Dark Victory* (1939).

All ► About

1939 is known as an exceptional year for exceptional films. *Juarez* was one of them. It starred Bette Davis as Carlotta of Mexico, who was driven insane after her husband Maximillian, Napoleon's brother, played by Paul Muni, was executed. John Garfield was featured in the decidedly offbeat characterization of Mexican General Diaz, and Claude Rains lent his considerable talents to the role of Napolean III. These elaborate pieces captured the look of Carlotta's European background and yet reveal an undercurrent of Latin influence and grace.

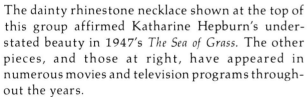

The dainty rhinestone necklace shown at the top of this group affirmed Katharine Hepburn's understated beauty in 1947's *The Sea of Grass.* The other pieces, and those at right, have appeared in numerous movies and television programs throughout the years.

Joseff on the set of *Forever Amber* with Linda Darnell. Note snake pieces on dressing table, described below.

This magnificent snake design was most effective when rendered in solid gold. Although the film was *Down to Earth*, (1947) it's doubtful Rita Hayworth could have kept both feet solidly grounded while wearing a necklace and bracelet of such graceful yet predisposing beauty.

Both of these necklaces were worn by Linda Darnell in *Forever Amber*, the 1947 film adapted from Kathleen Windsor's risque novel about intrigue in the court of Charles II.

A blonde Linda Darnell wears necklace shown on opposite page in this scene with George Sanders.

Three necklaces of varying genre. All used in many films, the one on the right specifically designed for *Forever Amber*.

A sand castle adds Old World ambiance to this brooch and pendant necklace worn by Viveca Lindfors in *The Adventures of Don Juan* (1948), with Don Juan portrayed by who else but Errol Flynn! Both were worn again in 1953 by the versatile Gladys Cooper in *Sons of the Musketeers*.

The efforts of director Michael Curtiz in preparing Errol Flynn for his role in *Captain Blood* are generally acknowledged to being paramount in making Flynn a star.

This filigree brooch of pearls and a center red cabochon was worn as a pendant by Viveca Lindfors in 1948's *The Adventures of Don Juan*, which was its "second-time around" ...Jeanette MacDonald wore it in 1936 in *Rose Marie*.

Errol Flynn once described himself thus.... "I allow myself to be known as a colorful fragment in a drab world."[3] He was certainly that in 1948's *The Adventures of Don Juan*, and these Joseff necklaces helped create the image and certainly contributed to the film garnering an Academy Award for Best Costumes.

Little wonder Errol Flynn found Viveca Lindfors irresistible in *The Adventures of Don Juan*. Her Joseff chatelaine and pendant add to her charm—and regal bearing.

From *Samson and Delilah*, a crown with magnificent center cabochon.

These massive pieces were certainly not "lost" on the screen when they appeared in *Lost Horizon* (1937).

This crown features the lion of Babylonia, a most appropriate design for *Samson and Delilah*, the 1949 movie starring Hedy Lamarr and Victor Mature, which not coincidentally won an Oscar for Best Costumes. A youthful Angela Lansbury portrayed Lamarr's older sister in the film.

There was a sharp edge to the roles portrayed in *The Women* in 1939, and Joseff skillfully captured the aura in this "up the arm" bracelet, designed to be worn by Joan Crawford over an elbow-length glove.

Wide cuff bracelet and dangling disc earrings worn by Maureen O'Hara in *Bagdad* (1949), where she portrayed the willful daughter of an Arab shiek.

Two very interesting jeweled pieces, known as "cleavagels," were ingeniously devised to cover some of the exposed bosom censors considered inappropriate for the eyes of the public—in this case they strategically adorned the bustlines of gowns worn by Lana Turner (at right) and Angela Lansbury (at left) in 1948's *The Three Musketeers.*

These pieces have seen quadruple duty! The coin jewelry first appeared on Adele Jergens in *A Thousand and One Nights* (1945), was also worn by Margaret Wycherly in *The Loves of Carmen* (1948) (with the filigree earrings appearing on Rita Hayworth in the same film), and the parure once again made an appearance when it complemented Maureen O'Hara's charms in *Bagdad* (1949).

Lana Turner and Gene Kelly in a scene from the 1948 version of *The Three Musketeers*.

This pendant necklace, shown on the dashing Douglas Fairbanks, Jr. in *Sinbad the Sailor* (1947), occupied an exceptionally prominent spot in the film, and was worn almost constantly by its star.

In this shot from *Sinbad the Sailor* (1947), Anthony Quinn is magnificently attired as the Emir who risks all in his search for the treasures of Alexander the Great.

101

CENTR CC101

ORCHESTRA
Loew's Grand Theatre
Friday Evening, Dec. 15, 1939

LOEW'S GRAND THEATRE
World Premiere of
GONE WITH THE WIND
Sponsored by the
ATLANTA COMMUNITY FUND
Friday, December 15, 1939 · 8:15 p. m.
Admission Price: Ten Dollars per ticket
Tax Exempt

SUNDAY, APRIL 28
Row W—Right
Seat 2

ROSELAND THEATRE, PANA, ILL.
Sunday, April 28, 1940—8 P. M.
"Gone With The Wind"
Admission $1.00; Fed. Tax 10c—Total $1.10

An original ticket for the gala premiere of *Gone With the Wind* in Atlanta on December 15, 1939.

Even the small theatres had special tickets with reserved seating for this stellar movie event. Dated Sunday, April 28, 1940 this one was for the Roseland Theatre in Pana, Illinois.

102

Scene V
"Gone With The Wind"

One of Joseff's most noteworthy assignments, and undeniably the *piece de resistance*, was to lend his talents to creating jeweled masterpieces for this century's most renowned epic...*Gone with the Wind*. He collaborated with his friend Walter Plunkett, the appointed costume designer, to produce original designs and to also convert Plunkett's "vision" of the historically appropriate jewelry into a finished "gem"!

Few, if any, films before or since have generated the pre- and post-production hype of this sweeping panorama of the Civil War South, nor has any novel ever raised the public's imagination to such heights of expectation. They were not destined to be disappointed!

Born in Atlanta in 1900, its author Margaret Mitchell was a product of the Civil War's aftermath, spending her childhood in an environment where veterans and ordinary citizens, who were still part of the lifeblood of the city, vividly recalled the War's horrors, as well as the genteel life they had lived in the Old South before the turmoil of the 1860s. Trips to the countryside revealed once stately mansions standing barren and desolate, ghostlike reminders of the devastation of fifty years before. It was these stories and images, indelibly imbedded in young Margaret's memory, that formed the basis of an untitled novel, written as a form of diversion when she was bedridden for many months in the 1920s with a broken, arthritic ankle.

Mitchell penned the last chapter first, and randomly added others. Except for three chapters, the book was completed in 1929, but with no intention on the part of the author to submit the manuscript for possible publication. Writing it had simply been an exercise to occupy Mitchell's time—and perhaps subconsciously serve as a medium for her flow of childhood images to take another, more material, form.

A series of seemingly unrelated circumstances culminated in her displeasure when a casual acquaintance remarked that the quiet Margaret didn't seem the type to write a book, and then coyly commented, "And you've never even been refused by a publisher. I've been refused by the very best."[1] This prompted Mitchell to turn the manuscript over to Macmillan and Company, which had previously been told of the book but couldn't convince her to allow their representative to evaluate it. At that point, Mitchell's purpose was simply to prove that she too could be rejected by one of the best! But there *was* no rejection, and this timeless saga of war and romance was eventually published in 1936. The rest is entertainment history.

In the rich tradition of the South, Mitchell's novel crossed all barriers in terms of audience appeal. North and South, East and West, nationwide and worldwide, it became an instant best seller. The working title was *Tomorrow Is Another Day*, but the author's personal choice was a phrase from the poem "Cynara" by Ernest Dowson—and *Gone with the Wind* it became! Although she tried to dissuade him, firmly believing it wasn't filmable, rights to the book were ultimately purchased by David O. Selznick, Louis B. Mayer's son-in-law, for a mere $50,000.

The search for actors and actresses to play the major roles generated a nationwide publicity frenzy of monumental proportions, including polls by newspapers, magazines, and even the studio, encouraging the public to vote for their favorites. Actresses of such stature as Joan Crawford, Tallulah Bankhead, Paulette Goddard, Norma Shearer, Jean Arthur, and even Lucille Ball, were considered and rejected. Disappointment had its compensations, however. "To console her when she lost the part of Scarlett O'Hara in *Gone with the Wind*. Charlie Chaplin gifted Paulette Goddard with a pair of cabochon emerald and diamond clips and matching bangle bracelet."[2] The bracelet alone recently fetched over $90,000 at Sotheby's!

Regardless of the charms of her many competitors, it now seems impossible that anyone *but* Vivian Leigh could have played Scarlett with the same nuances of seemingly fragile southern womanhood coupled with such fiery determination and haunting beauty. Selznick was captivated by that ethereal beauty at their first meeting, which took place during the filming of one of the scenes depicting Atlanta in flames, when Scarlett's role still remained to be cast. Selznick's brother Myron, who had previously met Leigh and been captivated by her, had chosen this dramatic moment for the introduction. He kept tugging at David Selznick's arm, imploring him to turn around and meet his leading lady at last. Although upset by the intrusion in the midst of this crucial scene, Selznick reluctantly did so, and for that he must have been everlastingly grateful. The story goes that the shadows of flames flickering across Leigh's face left no doubt. She *was* Scarlett—and after long months of frustration, *Gone with the Wind* had found its star!

Although her British heritage was far removed from the culture of the deep South—and the choice was certainly a courageous one and a box office gamble—Leigh and Scarlett were psychically intertwined, just as only Gable was uncannily Rhett. Who else could have given the rich and complex character of Rhett such a roguish exterior, generously laced with smoldering, mature sensuality and youthful vulnerability? The pairing was box office dynamite and the ultimate in flawless casting. Little wonder that the novel—and the film that meticulously captured its every detail—each remain as imbedded in the public consciousness today as they were fifty years ago!

Walter Plunkett, shown in drawing above, and his original watercolor sketches from *Gone with the Wind*. No words are needed.

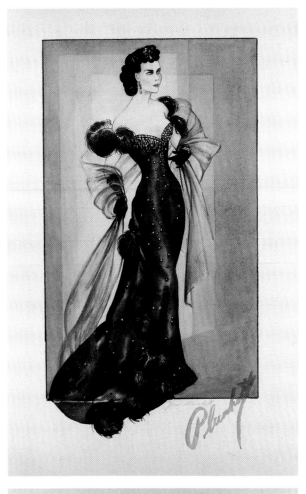

Although the female roles were competitively vied for by a bevy of Hollywood actresses, such was not the case when it came to the part of Rhett Butler. Nearly 100 percent of those polled felt that Clark Gable was perfect for the male lead. However, he had no interest whatsoever in the role. "It wasn't that I didn't appreciate the compliment the public was paying me," he said. "It was simply that Rhett was too big an order. I didn't want any part of him....Rhett was too much for any actor to tackle in his right mind."3

The signing of Gable for *Gone with the Wind* involved more than polls and popularity, however. Louis B. Mayer loaned Clark Gable to his son-in-law David Selznick on the condition that the film be released through MGM. "So in 1939, MGM had gotten itself the biggest money-maker in Hollywood history without having to invest a penny of its own money."4

Selznick was a stickler for having every detail correct, and the film is generally acknowledged to be historically accurate down to the most minute details. For instance, the "damn" in Rhett Butler's parting line to Scarlett is an expression of the day, "a tinker's dam," and referred to a small piece of clay placed around the hole in a pot to prevent the solder from running off while the vessel was being repaired. So Rhett wasn't blasphemous after all—but the publicity it generated in those days of strict Hays Office censorship certainly enhanced rather than harmed the film's image! Surprisingly, and to the regret of film buffs and *Gone with the Wind* enthusiasts everywhere, this final scene between Scarlett and Rhett is one of the few in the entire picture for which no black and white stills were taken.

Frank Nugent's New York Times review of *Gone with the Wind* read, in part, "Had we space we'd talk about...the dramatic use to which Mr. Fleming has paced his Technicolor—although we still feel that color is hard on the eyes for so long a picture—and about pictures of this length in general."5 The reaction of audiences for over fifty years has certainly belied this grim assessment!

Every detail of the film, both before and after release, came under scrutiny and was considered newsworthy. In describing one of Scarlett's gowns, a publicity caption read: "...a striking gown of burgundy velvet ornamented with scattered garnets, and trimmed with wine-colored ostrich tips, which extend to the hem. A veil of wine tulle and three-quarter length gloves of the same color; garnets in gold mountings for bracelet and earrings complete the ensemble."6 Sadly, although John Frederics was commissioned to design all the hats for the film, and meticulously completed the assignment, none of them ever appeared in the movie.

Because of the length and scope of the book, which covered three historical fashion periods, Walter Plunkett determined that there could conceivably be as many as 5,500 different costumes necessary to complete the film! A mammoth undertaking, as was that of the production designer William Cameron Menzies. In the end, not counting the uniforms, 2,868 costumes had to be made.

The screenwriter was Sidney Howard, a Pulitzer Prize-winning playwright, whose initial script was four hundred pages and would have culminated in a movie over five hours in length. Selznick later called on writers of such stature as Charles MacArthur (husband of Helen Hayes), F. Scott Fitzgerald, and John Van Druten to lend their expertise in making alterations, but little of useable value was forthcoming.

A swan boat majestically carries the necklace worn by Scarlett in the scene from *Gone With the Wind* where she confesses her love to an unsuspecting Ashley.

George Cukor was originally hired as director, but very shortly after initial filming took place, he departed and Victor Fleming was chosen to replace him. Fleming, unhappy with the script—which was still incomplete—insisted that he was unavailable unless a completed draft reached his hands before the start date. At that point, Ben Hecht was called in and, returning to Howard's original drafts, days and weeks of feverish work by the trio of Selznick, Fleming and Hecht brought the script into somewhat makeshift order.

In the end, in light of his pioneering work on this monumental undertaking, it was decided to give final credit for the screenplay to Howard, who tragically had been killed in a tractor accident on his farm in Massachusetts a month prior to the premiere. The art director was Lyle Wheeler. The magnificent musical score was by Max Steiner.

Well into the filming, Fleming suddenly pleaded that he was "suffering a nervous breakdown," and disappeared from the set. No one knew when to expect his return, if ever! During his mysterious absence, Sam Wood was hired as interim director, which worked to the film's advantage after Fleming rejoined the company, since one director would shoot scenes in the morning, the other in the afternoon. However, because it was felt that Fleming had made the most extensive and valuable contribution, his name was the sole one to appear in the final credits.

Originally cut to four-and-a-half hours for its preview showings, which were met with overwhelming enthusiasm, *Gone with the Wind* was still thought to be too long for audience comfort. An intermission was added, and the final length reduced to 3 hours and 45 minutes—probably the most memorable 3 hours and 45 minutes ever captured on film!

Belle Watling and her bell earrings.

The magic of the movies reaches its apex once one has viewed and held these pieces: Clark Gable's cigar case from *Gone with the Wind* and the necklace Scarlett wore on her honeymoon to New Orleans with Rhett. The case was designed with interchangeable plates so that it would appear to be two separate pieces. In one movie still, it can be seen lying on top of a donation basket full of metal objects being collected for the war effort. While Rhett looks on, Melanie is stoically removing her wedding ring to add to the meager but courageous contributions. Joan Joseff continues to be hounded by women who simply want to touch the case—most of whom then vow never to wash their hands again!

Young Eugene. Probably a parochial school photograph.

Eugene Joseff shortly before he left Chicago to seek his fortune in Hollywood.

Scene VI
A Family Gallery

Joseff looking decidedly different in a mustache he sported for several years.

A later Joseff portrait.

Joan Castle Joseff in several glamorous poses that personify the aura of the 1940s.

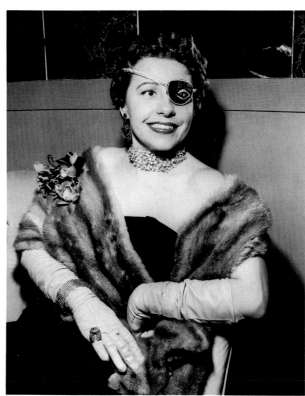

Undaunted by an eye injury that followed on the heels of a skiing accident, Joan fashioned this exotic eye patch covered with genuine gems!

The dapper Walter Plunkett—Joseff's friend and mentor.

A celebration at the first Mardi Gras after the War! This photo was taken at The Old Absinthe House in New Orleans. Proprietor Owen Brennan is at the head of the table. To his left is Joseff, to his right Elliott Roosevelt and his wife Faye Emerson. Joan is in front, wearing the feathered hat. Her best friend and husband are seated across from her. Hats were an important accessory in the 1940s, as the chapeaus in this photo testify.

Friend "Prince" Mike Romanoff poses with a Joseff crown and a disdainful look befitting his "royal" position.

Joseff gives Mike Romanoff a "run for his money" in the "most stately prince" contest!

In this Joseff publicity release from 1948, the caption reads, "Joseff has a first name but he will not reveal it. He holds a collection of simulated diamonds and is surrounded by costume pieces that he rents to Hollywood studios. The jewelled belt at the left was first worn by Rudolph Valentino."

Another release, also from 1948, read: "Costume pieces are not melted down after use. They are photographed to make sure none of the stones are missing, then catalogued library style." This show-room/office remains much the same today.

Busy! Busy! Busy! Here Joseff gets a haircut while going over the checklist before takeoff.

Joseff and Joan, holding newborn Jeff.

Joseff, Joan, and friends pose happily in front of their private plane.

118

Joan's unique bird cage ring inspired copies. The left one plays up the cupid theme, the one on the right encased a faux jewel!

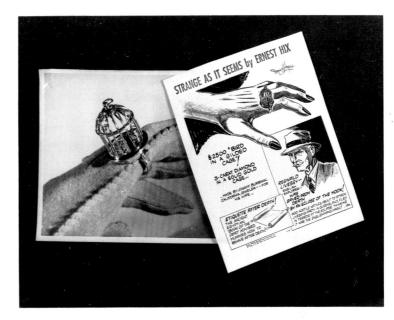

Ernest Hix's *Strange as it Seems* column featuring Joan's birdcage ring. (Shortly after, Hix lost his life in plane crash with Joseff).

Joan and the tree both glitter at one of the famous Christmas parties.

A "Daliesque" oil painting captures the harlequin and magician in Eugene Joseff. Joan is depicted behind him in surreal imagery.

The dapper and handsome Joseff poses in front of his harlequin portrait.

Joan Joseff today in the office used by both her and Joseff.

121

Joseff, Jeweler to the Stars and You

Jane Russell with acorn cluster brooch and ear- rings.

IT is odd that one of the newest of man's arts should help to revive one of the oldest of man's arts! That is what the movie camera has done to jewelry. Where the theatre tended to develop a "general effect" school of baubles, and social life has a "how big and how real is it?" standard about jewelry, the camera has demanded that jewelry be beautifully designed, perfectly executed. It doesn't care whether the stones are paste, the metals rare or base. The design and workmanship are all-important. Those were the oldest and first tests applied to jewelry. They are the tests now used by Joseff, jeweler to the stars.

Why are these standards important for the camera? Most obviously because of the close-up technique, where the head (and necklace, brooch, and earrings) of the heroine is virtually in your lap. In these shots, it is the small amount of jewelry plus a coiffure and make-up that must convey to you all that entire costumes and settings do on the stage. And jewelry for the movies must do all of this, without attracting too much attention away from the star's expression and acting.

Small wonder that Hollywood took to itself a young artist who really understood the camera requirements of jewelry for a star . . . a man who could create pieces that would re-inforce an actress's rôle, and "stand inspection" under the almost microscopic eyes of the camera. Remember the star pendant Bette Davis wore on that scandalous red dress in *Jezebel?* Remember the aura of lavishness that surrounded Norma Shearer in *Marie Antoinette*..."

Scene VII
Joseff Jewels for Everyone

Movies of the 1930s and 1940s had drastically influenced more than our sociological and psychological mores, however. On a more simple, basic level they created distinct changes in what women, and men, desired—and purchased. Or, in some cases, didn't purchase!

When Clark Gable removed his shirt in *It Happened One Night* to reveal nothing between it and his bare chest, the men's underwear industry suffered a severe and long-standing blow to their sales figures. Similarly, when a shoe manufacturer supplied the footwear for *Exile Express*, not knowing that the script called for Anna Sten's feet to be the source of grimacing pain, the "plug," although somewhat amusing, became a source of much embarrassment to the maker.

On the plus side, sales of chenille robes skyrocketed when Deanna Durbin wore one in 1939's *Three Smart Girls Grow Up* and there was a rush to order "French" telephones when audiences saw stars like Rosalind Russell using them. In 1937 the kerchief industry got an unexpected sales bonanza because Joan Crawford tied one around her head in *The Bride Wore Red*. Milliners were hit hard, however, when women found more and more occasions to replace hats with kerchiefs, scarves, and knit and lace "fascinators."

What we saw on the screen in that golden era also affected what we drank, smoked and drove. Products like Lucky Strikes, Coca Cola, Cadillacs, Chevys and Packards benefited by exposure in the movies, and sales of pink champagne soared when Irene Dunne and Charles Boyer romantically gazed into each other's eyes while sipping it in 1939's *Love Affair*.

Joseff, who also designed jewelry for the personal wardrobes of stars like Carole Lombard, Myrna Loy, Alice Faye, Norma Shearer, Jeanette MacDonald, Janet Gaynor, and Constance Bennett, was astute enough to realize that by owning the styles of jewelry they admired on screen beauties of the day, and knowing they were made by the man who designed those pieces they coveted in their favorite films, created a ready retail market for his creations. Joseff was also

Opposite page:
Portion of an article on Joseff from *Glamour* magazine in the early 1940s. It later went on to reinforce Joseff's retail philosophy, "...for movies, for stars, and for you."

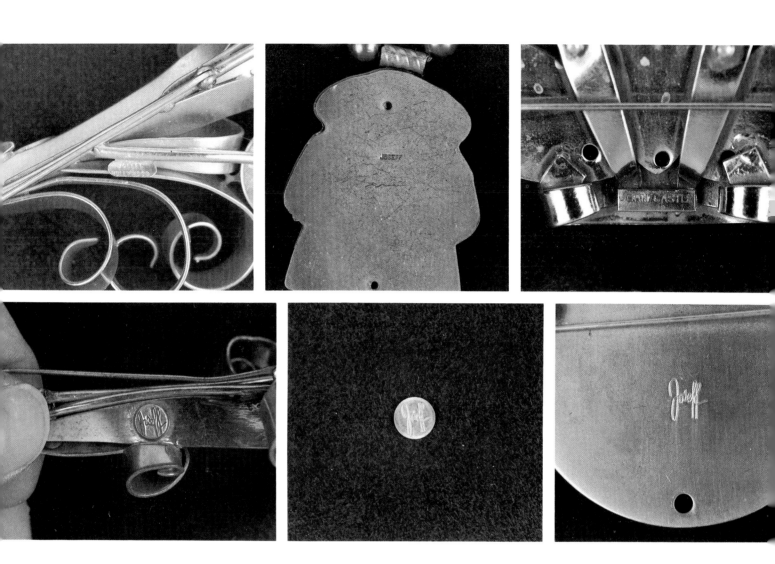

Joseff logos

aware of the impact his own "jewels" could have if offered to the American woman in exclusive settings within the framework of top department stores and boutiques. He had little difficulty in generating enthusiasm among retail outlets for a jewelry line of high-quality, unusual pieces that reflected his expertise in the glamour of film, and he wisely decided to limit the number of stores in which this jewelry would be featured to only five hundred, scattered throughout the United States. Among these were such exclusive giants as B. Altman, Bullocks, Julius Garfinkel, Pogues, Neiman-Marcus, Wanamaker's, and Marshall Field.

Designating others to handle the merchandising of this new venture would have seemed only logical, especially with the movie side of the business continuing at such a breakneck pace. But for Eugene Joseff this expansion became a very personal mission and his involvement was paramount to its success. He believed that women were entitled to more than an impersonal viewing of costume pieces through the glass of a department store jewelry counter. Their ultimate presentation involved sophistication and theatrics. They were designed to make women feel special, to make them not only confident in their accessorizing abilities, but glamorous and desirable—just like the beautiful heroines they admired in the movies!

The success of this new jewelry line was a public relations triumph, calling upon Joseff's background in advertising and his innate abilities as a showman and entrepreneur. But most importantly, all of these skills were coupled with a genuine desire to give the American woman something new and exciting, and to present it in a manner that conveyed her own sense of importance.

It was during this time that flying became a passion with Joseff and, like everything else in his life, he threw himself wholeheartedly into his hobby, quickly becoming an accomplished pilot. Sitting at the controls of his own plane opened new vistas. It was perhaps the ultimate expression of Joseff's adventurous and independent nature, and he incorporated his skill into an unusual merchandising tool.

Piloting his plane to hopscotch from one city to the next on promotional tours to stores throughout the country became a common occurrence for Joseff. He enjoyed this diversion from the sometimes jaded atmosphere of Hollywood, charming customers and store personnel with his urbane mannerisms and wit.

JC, although at first reluctant, eventually enjoyed these airborne jaunts, and Joseff set about teaching her to fly. Although a special camaraderie took place thousands of feet above the earth, JC laughingly recalls one particular instance when he wasn't pleased with his pupil's aeronautical skills. With Joseff shouting directions that she, at least to his mind, failed to comprehend, JC in utter frustration finally screamed, "Take the damned controls yourself!" They reached a truce once their feet were on the ground and joked about it afterwards. But up there in the "wild blue yonder" teacher and student were just that!

An article in the January, 1938 issue of *California Stylist* makes it clear that Joseff was very influential in molding concepts and trends for the retail jewelry market. He is quoted as saying:

> Attempts at Cellini's mastery of barbaric gold working will be made...to adorn the well dressed lady of 1938....There will be larger and more barbaric necklaces, bracelets, brooches, and even the flattering long ear drops will have their chance....There will be transparent fruit, brightly colored wooden novelties that make all former attempts look dull.

And so, Cellini continued to play a posthumous role in the work of Eugene Joseff—as did the exclusive lost wax process, attributed to Cellini, that he employed in his castings.

On the same subject, Joseff went on to say:

> There will be large flowers, bunches of varicolored grapes and cherries. Novelty will be brought out in the design, for instead of being carved of one large block, large jewelry slides will be featured on all types of jewelry, including belts. Leather necklaces studded with jewels and gold will be in vogue. English silver will hold preference over gold for sportswear. Finer designs for formal wear will follow the seventeenth century vogue for minute paste stones and diamonds....

Joseff personally designed many of the artistic window displays featuring his jewelry. He also wrote specialty columns and was the subject of countless articles in major movie magazines and newspapers. A portion of one of those articles, excerpted from the February 1948 issue of *Movie Show* magazine, is an insightful glimpse into Joseff's philosophy on accessorizing with jewelry, and his clever adaptation of this theory into eye-catching window arrangements designed to draw the observer's eye to specific pieces in a very calculated order.

> When you want to buy jewelry, you should first know how much you want to spend. Then be guided by the type of clothes you wear, and where you wear them....
>
> If you want to acquire a collection, start with a brooch because you will find most use for it. It can be pinned on a suit lapel, collar or pocket...on a hat, a belt, or an evening gown. Remember, gold can be worn with more things than silver and topaz is a good stone that looks smart with almost every type of costume....
>
> Earrings should be the next jewelry investment. They also have many uses. You can wear them on your hat, cuffs, shoes, as well as on your ears.
>
> A ring comes next in your collection and I'd suggest finding a bold ring with a large stone...something massive and distinctive. A bracelet and a necklace come last in importance because they can so seldom be worn with all your costumes or for all occasions.
>
> Keep in mind the fact that jewelry is an accent that draws the eye. With a necklace, earrings and hat or hair ornament, the eye is forced to encircle the face. If you have lovely hands, a bracelet or ring will draw attention to them. A belt buckle, or a pin worn at the waistline, will make people notice a slender waist. Put a pair of buckles on your slippers if you want people to see your small feet.
>
> Just be careful to keep the one important piece of jewelry in one area, to focus attention there. Otherwise, if you use too much jewelry in a scattered way, the eye zigzags without getting any particular impression.
>
> We follow these principles when we place jewelry in a store window. We can put fifty pieces in a window in such a way that the eye will start at one point, go around the case and finally focus on one particular item.

Joseff is greeted by Buffums' representative on one of his airborne promotional jaunts.

These intricate pieces capture the romantic influence of Victorian times.

Some years later Joan added her own sage advice. "Think of your jewelry as part of your makeup.... Combine antique and modern jewelry, just as you would your furniture. Don't be hesitant to use gold and silver together." In numerous articles of the day she was quoted as making several statements that might appear somewhat controversial but certainly conveyed Joan's own sense of style. One was that pearls were unimaginative, and the other was that "...wearing school jewelry, like a class ring, indicates that the individual is probably hanging onto the past, or is afraid of the future." JC's degree in psychology was exerting an influence even in the jewelry business!

Using the trademark "Joseff, Jeweller to the Stars" to marvelous advantage, Joseff wanted women everywhere to know that they too were *stars*! The success he achieved was well deserved, for he and Joan had created an exciting new promotional concept in the fashion jewelry field.

However, it took Eugene Joseff, with his personable countenance and entrepreneurial "know-how" to bring it all together. Joseff's diversified background enabled him to package his skills in a spellbinding manner and to present jewelry with a "motion picture flair" to a mass audience. Indeed, who but Eugene Joseff has ever earned the distinction of being recognized as the "Jeweller to the Stars"? And who but Eugene Joseff carried this star connection directly to the American woman?

A portion of an April 1938 *Women's Wear Daily* article about Joseff reads, "Joseff, the designer of jewelry for motion pictures, is now reproducing certain of his designs for the trade. Among the favorites are his 'head hunter' pin in jet black with gold ring in the nose and ears." The April 1938 *Mademoiselle Advance Fashion Report* states:

> A new jewelry resource that is attracting much attention...is headed by Joseff, who has made a unique reputation designing and renting jewelry for motion picture productions. Copies of famous antique pieces and designs are made to order. Be sure to see his charm necklaces....

Whether on the screen or at retail jewelry counters in fine stores throughout the United States, Joseff jewelry was alternately delicate and bold, but always feminine. Eager buyers of the retail line had an intriguing assortment to choose from. One thing was clear. *Jewelery by Joseff* was never nondescript! Regardless of the buyer's choice, it made a statement on their behalf. Even the more tailored pieces displayed unique attributes in design and finish, as can be seen in the astrological brooches and earrings. There was an added bonus to these pieces, as well, for the women who chose them felt a sense of individuality when they purchased and wore their own "sign." It was a marketing masterpiece. Just one of many in the Joseff repertoire.

But what set this particular retail venture apart from many other unique marketing successes was Joseff's sincere devotion to what he was presenting, how he was presenting it, and most importantly the women he was presenting it to!

Jewelry by Joseff will be worn
by models in The Tea Room today and next week.

BULLOCK'S • BROADWAY • HILL • SEVENTH

These 1939 Bullock's color ads (probably two of the first of their kind) featured Joseff jewelry "to be shown in the Tea Room." This genteel atmosphere was certainly a far cry from the teeming malls of today.

Tassel brooch designed by Joseff for the personal wardrobe of Gail Patrick, Paramount star. Some movie pieces later were converted to retail designs, and others, designed specifically for the personel wardrobes of actresses also became retail items.

Adapted from the cape fastener designed by Joseff for Greta Garbo's *Camille,* and also worn by Olivia deHaviland in *Robin Hood,* this one was for Glenda Farrell's personal wardrobe and later became a retail item.

The more the merrier! This lariat necklace, a Joseff exclusive, was originally designed for the personal wardrobe of Constance Bennett and later adapted for the retail line. Available in one, two, three, or four strands, it was photographed here on then starlet Rita Hayworth.

Antique cross, adaptation of a Renaissance piece in the Metropolitan Museum, was originally designed for Loretta Young to wear in the Twentieth Century-Fox picture *Wife, Doctor and Nurse.* Miss Young was so enthusiastic about the piece that she ordered it for herself and had three more made as gifts for friends. Photographed on June Lang.

Early retail pieces, all with the distinctive Joseff finish. The acorns form a unique lariat.

Three early brass retail pieces. All assertive. All beautiful and unique!

Even a parrot couldn't resist these Joseff pieces—
from Mayan figures to pearls, cabochons and onyx
dangles, all made a statement that women adored.

Two bar brooches, once again much in style, flank
three glorious brooches—all early retail pieces, their
quality graphically attested to by these beautiful
stones, undimmed by time!

A cross-section of Joseff pieces.
All are different; all are beautiful
and unique.

An array of early Joseff retail pieces surround a feathered hair piece.

This crown pendant was designed for the popular radio program "Queen for a Day." (See above)

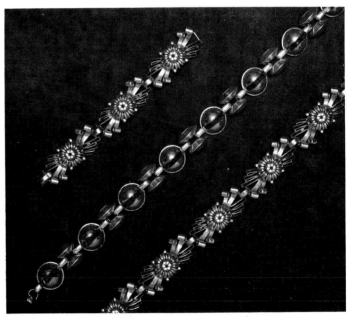

Stunning in design, an intricate necklace and bracelet flank a necklace of gold balls, each centered with brilliant red stones.

This publicity shot for another variation of the turban necklace had an appropriately attired gentleman superimposed on the photo.

Constance Moore wears companion brooch to the turban head necklace.

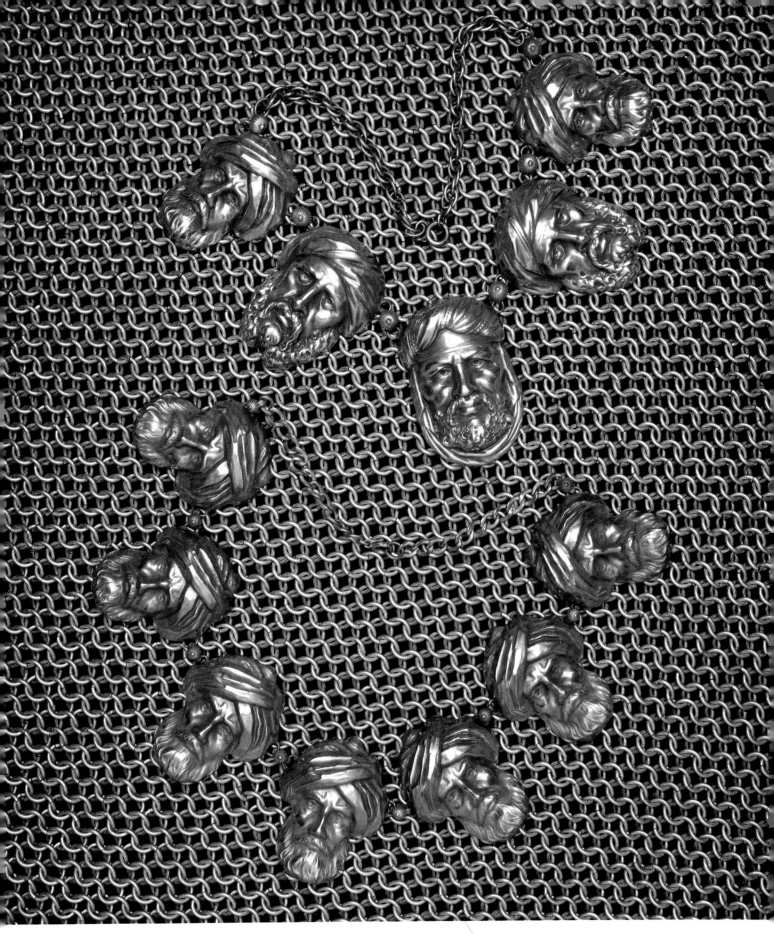

These giant turban-headed necklaces were retail
"traffic-stoppers"!

This huge gold leaf brooch with cabochon amethyst center can also be worn as a hair clip.

A money tree brooch from the 1950s.

And here's Maureen O'Hara wearing it!

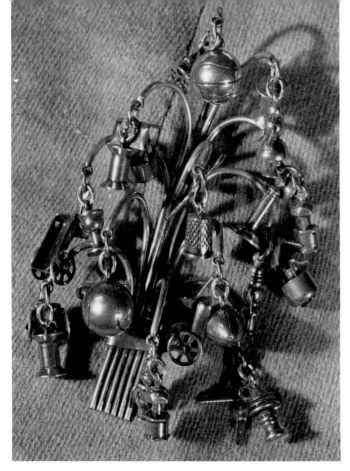

Along the same lines as the money tree, this tree is laden with whimsical charms.

Priscilla Lane, another of the three Lane sisters, wearing brooch similar to the group below.

Incomparable! The special finish on Joseff's early brass pieces made each brooch a symphony of design!

137

Joseff admiring parure on
Kathleen Wilson, radio soap-
opera star.

Jean Parker wears the Renaissance cross designed for her role in *Arkansas Traveler* (1938) and later converted to the retail line.

A swan and her goslings, all with precious cargo—Joseff rings and an early Joseff retail brooch of fluttering flowers.

No "King Kong" here! This antique tassel necklace was designed for the personal wardrobe of a less rumpled Faye Wray.

A cartouche ornament, copy of an authentic antique, worn by soldiers on cartouche boxes. Created by Joseff for Olivia de Haviland to wear in the Warner Brother's production *Dodge City*, it was later adapted for the retail trade.

Three massive brooches and necklace show intricate detail of designs and are a tribute to the costume jeweler's art.

This lapel pin, worn by Ginger Rogers and later adapted for retail, was originally designed for Douglas Fairbanks, Jr., to wear in *Gunga Din* (see inset).

140

Three varied and ornate Joseff retail designs.

Bold Joseff pieces are companions to hanging leaves worn by a sophisticated model. Photographed in the 1940's tradition.

Two retail brooches of the same genre. The gigantic one on bottom also can be worn as a "show-stopping" pendant.

Gail Patrick wears an ivory version of the head-hunter brooch in this 1941 shot.

These retail brooches run the gamut from delicate flowers to the famous "headhunters."

This headhunter brooch with ring through the nose and tassel "earrings" was one of Joseff's most popular and unique retail designs.

The beauteous redhead Ann Sheridan wears a simple but dramatic Joseff creation.

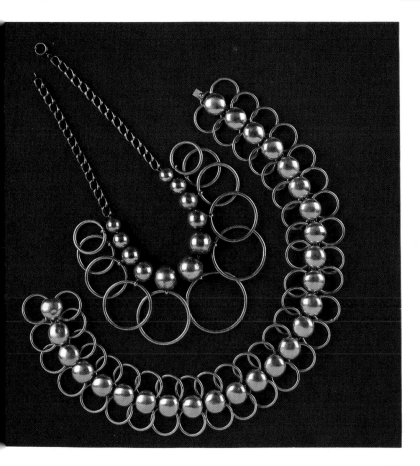

Joseff designed the personalized initials on Mary Dunhill lipstick cases.

Simple swirls of "gold" become elaborate symphonies of design.

The mysteries of the Middle East influenced these
Joseff designs.

Earrings on parade!

Evelyn Keyes in a glamorous shot—wearing a glamorous choker!

Joseff's seashell necklace (one of a series of shell and sea creatures designs) complements Virginia Mayo's sun dress.

Filigree drum necklace designed by Joseff for Constance Bennett to wear in the Universal production *Service Deluxe*. Later adapted for retail.

Anne Shirley (the girl Bob Hope sang "Thanks for the Memory" to) in a photo that has everything—'40s upswept brim hat, pompadour hairdo, the always proper gloves, a large satchel handbag, and Joseff's funky, but practical, key brooch.

Larraine Day, always a wholesome beauty, wearing a necklace inspired by the many jungle epics featuring Joseff baubles.

Swinging Buddha designed by Joseff for Evelyn Knapp to wear in *Wanted by the Police*.

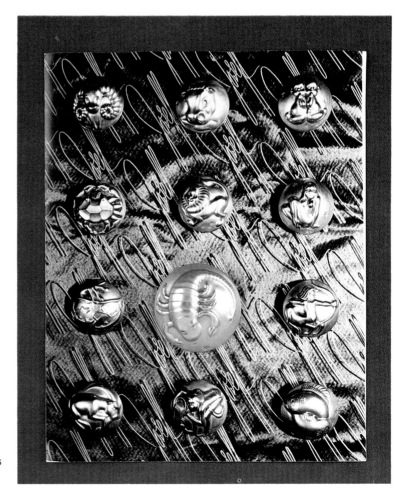

The scorpion sits amid fellow astrological pieces assembled for a Joseff promotional photograph.

Gale Page wearing Joseff lariat necklace and bracelet for her role in *Four Wives* (1940).

Early design drawings for Joseff retail jewelry.

149

Rosemary Lane, sister of Priscilla and Lola, wears the Joseff brooch shown in design photo at right and with gold and ruby bracelet below. The bracelet originally sold for $27 and the pin for $25.

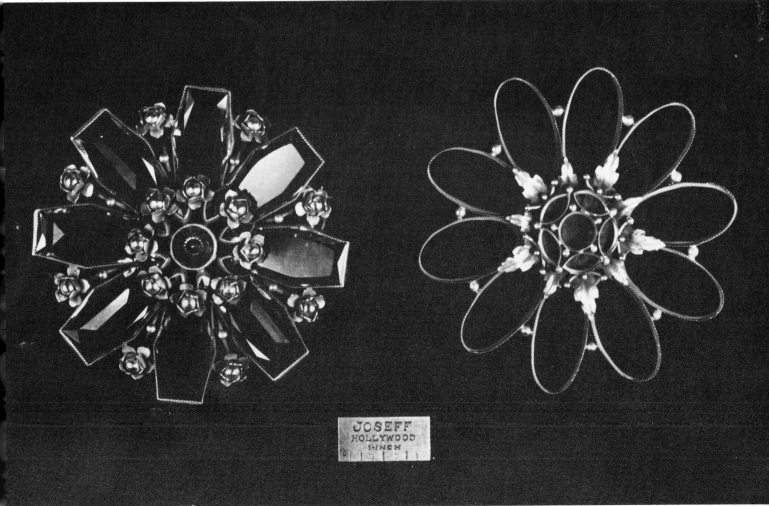

JOSEFF
HOLLYWOOD
1-INCH

151

These dynamic brooches are all early retail pieces.

Joseff was renowned for his cupids. These charming retail pieces elaborate on the Valentine's Day theme, with a dangling charm necklace and intricate cupid cuff, two cupid heart-theme brooches, and dangling cupid earrings.

A 1956 advertisement from the jewelry trade magazine *Jewelers Circular Keystone.* Note caption that reads, "Conversation pieces for the connoisseur."

Ann Robinson, Warner Bros. starlet, wearing Joseff set pictured in ad at left.

This page was from the 1938 magazine *Dress Accessories*, featuring Joseff jewelry.

Multicolored stones and mesh create a spectacular fashion statement in this gigantic bib and bracelet combination.

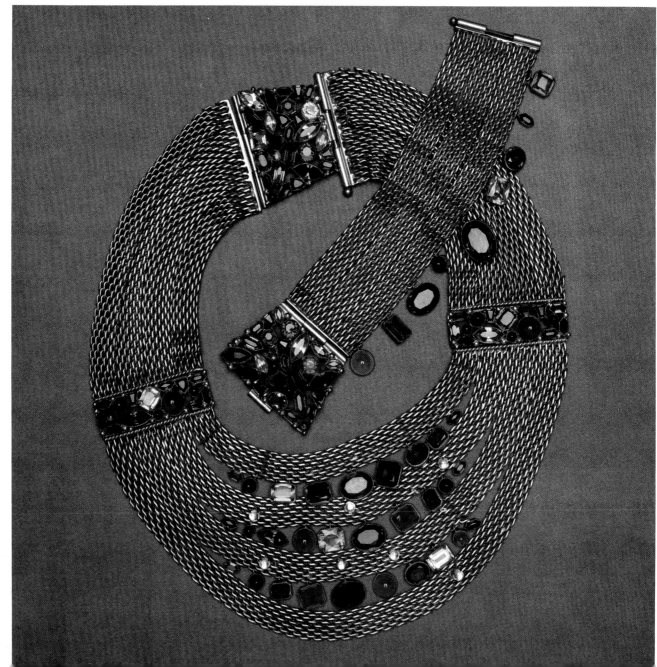

The beauty and innovation of Joseff design in a display window.

Mixing movies with retail in July 1938 a Bullock's
Los Angeles window showcased an elaborate gown
for the film *Marie Antoinette*.

A dynamic Joseff window display showcasing his
Oriental pieces to great advantage.

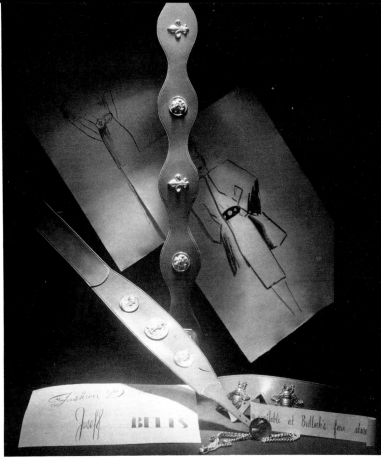

Joseff's window displays designed by Edward Boehme at Bullock's in Los Angeles were a source of personal pride. They reflected an artistic sense of style and merchandising expertise.

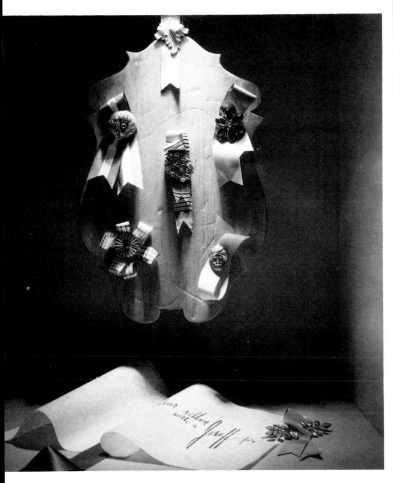

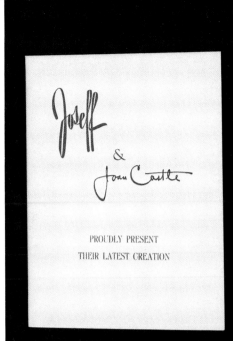

Joseff
&
Joan Castle

PROUDLY PRESENT
THEIR LATEST CREATION

Jeffrey Rene Joseff

premier

october 13, 1947   8:41 p.m.

6 lbs. 13 oz.

hollywood hospital

continuous showing
736 north brighton street, burbank, california

Scene VIII
Carrying the Dream Forward

Although JC had never considered herself the perfect candidate for motherhood, and approached the idea with some trepidation, Joseff was eager to have a child. On October 13, 1947, Jeffrey Rene Joseff was born, and her fears immediately washed away. They both adored him, and Joan found that adding the role of mother to her already "full plate" wasn't as difficult, or frightening, as she had imagined. The decision is one for which Joan has given thanks many times over the ensuing years, for she can never forget the joy this baby gave to her and Joseff in the few short months the three of them shared together.

In September, 1948 Joseff and JC had planned to fly to their newly-purchased ranch in Prescott, Arizona, a town where Joseff had also opened a jewelry boutique just two years before. They had spent many hours discussing details of the massive renovations they faced in order to restore this rundown 1876 "masterpiece" of the Old West to their "home away from home." Both envisioned Jeff playing amid the carefree, open spaces of their own ranch. But it was never to be.

Several days before the scheduled departure, a series of circumstances forced Joan to forego the trip. Joseff, anxious to share his new acquisition with three male friends, including Ernest Hix, author of the syndicated column "Strange as it Seems," invited them to join him for a "bachelors' weekend." On September 18, Joan took him to Newhall Airport where his plane was hangared, and with eleven month old Jeff in her arms said a fond goodbye and immediately drove home.

By mid-afternoon Joan had received several puzzling phone calls from friends. All asked basically the same question, alluding to what she was doing. In each case she replied that housekeeping and baby tending chores were keeping her busy as usual. The conversations were stilted and ended abruptly as the callers mumbled hasty good-byes. She soon found out why. The tragic story had been reported on the radio before the authorities could locate James Joseff and arm him with the heartbreaking task of telling her the unthinkable. Shortly after takeoff, Joseff's plane had crashed with no survivors. In exactly one week, Eugene Joseff would have celebrated his forty-third birthday.

An instant in time changed the idyllic fairy tale existence of Joan Castle Joseff into a nightmare. She grieved inconsolably for weeks—and soon the weeks turned into months. The usual tormenting questions that inevitably confront those left behind after such tragedies surfaced again and again. What if she had gone with him instead? Would the circumstances then have been different? Suppose she had taken the baby. The "what ifs" were endless.

And then, after months of depression and soul-searching, Joan suddenly realized that she had only two clear options for her future. She could continue grieving, or she could pick up the pieces and continue with the work she and Joseff had so carefully built. Joan knew he would have expected no less than the latter.

However, without her partner the business would have to be a somewhat different one, for only Joseff could give it that *special mystique* that had set him apart from the very beginning. On the other hand, they had a small but highly skilled staff who, under her careful supervision, could continue with the design and manufacture of Joseff movie pieces and the retail line, as well as the airplane parts end of the business, which had expanded after the war into contracts for commercial aircraft.

A half-page 1956 newspaper ad for the Joseff operation gives some indication of the dedication Joan had to that business and how successful she was in building upon the integrity and commitment of its founder. It read, in part:

> For twenty-five years now, we've been part and parcel of this wonderful hectic California way. We pioneered aircraft castings on the West Coast. We pioneered in castings for the electronic industry, too, and today we're the leading supplier in that field. We think that we've got the edge....We've got the plant. We've got the people. We've got the experience....and we'll break our necks to give you the best job and the best service you've ever had.

Joan Castle Joseff stands only five feet tall, but she has been blessed with fiery determination and an ability to turn almost certain defeat into personal victory. The life she had chosen wasn't all glamour. She had endured long, boring hours and seemingly endless days on movie sets, waiting patiently to assist with the Joseff jewelry that was to be used that day—or the next. On one exhausting occasion she'd returned to the factory at midnight, only to spend much of the night scrubbing raw meat from the chain mail they'd supplied for a jungle epic. The outwardly ferocious lion had turned into a pussycat and meat had to be smeared all over the mail to make him attack! This was the unglamorous side of the business. Regardless, those memories were precious. There was no question as to her decision. She owed it to Joseff to continue—and she owed it to herself to go forward.

Eugene Joseff was an amateur magician. He was fascinated by the spell that magic could weave and the artisanship necessary to make one a truly great master of legerdemain. To this day, Joan Joseff remains a member of that splendid bastion to the magician's art, The Magic Castle in Los Angeles. And to this day the Joseff magic remains, just as it did in those first uncertain times without him.

To keep the business going and provide a loving home for her son were her only priorities. It would have been well nigh impossible to do both if Joan's mother hadn't moved in and helped care for young Jeff. Nevertheless, while Joan struggled with reorganizing and strengthening the Joseff operation, the major responsibility of being both mother and father to her son fell mightily on her tiny but capable shoulders.

The company was not in good financial shape in 1948. Excess profit taxes and defense contract cutbacks following the war had eroded their earnings. Unexpected employee problems also surfaced in the wake of Joseff's death. JC's first step was to deal with these swiftly and decisively, and it was this hardheaded realism that kept the business solvent.

But there was another side to Joan Castle Joseff. That glimpse of another Joan was succinctly described in a quote some ten years later in a 1959 issue of *Star Weekly* magazine. "Jewelry and electronics are her business, but this glamorous tycoon in the French blue office confides she's built her success on charm. 'No man is going to forget I'm a woman,' she says." JC was indeed a refreshing beacon of femininity in a man's world!

When one examines the many press clippings from this period, there is little doubt that entrepreneurial skills weren't solely the domain of Eugene Joseff, for Joan's expertise in marketing jewelry and her own image as part of the "package" shine through. Indeed, it becomes apparent that Eugene Joseff and Joan Castle were more alike than either probably realized, merchandising skills not being the least of their similarities. Just as Joseff had incorporated himself as a highly visible part of their business, so did Joan after his death. She inherently recognized that her personal aura and enthusiasm created an environment in which the business would flourish. It is doubtful the effervescent Joan Joseff could have functioned in any other way. At the height of the recession of 1958-1959, who else would have designed a postage stamp-size card for past and present clients that read, in microscopic print, "Lack of orders from you has made this economy size card necessary"!

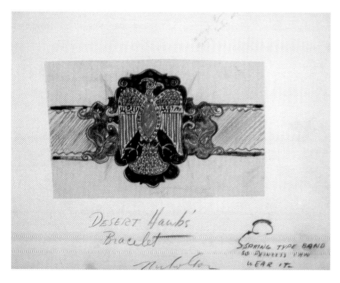

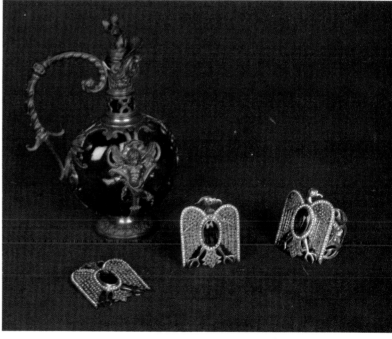

This massive bracelet and dual brooches complement the aura of the film...this one, *The Desert Hawk* (1950), starred the exotic Yvonne deCarlo and her handsome leading man Richard Greene.

It seems unlikely, considering the title, but Andrea King wore this in a 1949 film called *Buccaneer's Girl*, the plot of which revolved around two seemingly unrelated themes—piracy and New Orleans dance hall life!

Joan Joseff loves people. They fill her with vitality and she returns the favor! In those days of the 1950s and 1960s she was overflowing with energy and good cheer. Her annual Christmas parties became legend and were considered the official "kick off" to the festive holiday season. This was Joan's one big party of the year, and she was quoted as saying, "So I don't offend anyone, I invite everyone I know. It's easier that way." The "everyone I know" numbered anywhere from 600 to 1,000, all of whom received engraved invitations from Tiffany's. The Los Angeles Herald reported that "...Next year she may need the Coliseum."

As an article in *The Citizens News* observed in 1958, Joan mixed her guest list like "an imaginative bartender." They ran the gamut from movie stars and fashion designers to aircraft moguls. In 1960, one newspaper reporter watched awestruck as Mary Pickford and Buddy Rogers descended the staircase to the Crystal Room of the Beverly Hills Hotel hand in hand!

The parties were overflowing with the Joseff sense of heady fun...and holiday tradition. Until 1960, when she switched to the larger facilities at the Beverly Hills Hotel, the Yuletide "bash" was held at Romanoff's. Year after year the focal point of the evening put this particular holiday extravaganza squarely ahead of any other. It was a Christmas tree unequaled in splendor and value. The tree itself varied in style, size, and theme, but one thing was a certainty—it would be covered with half a million dollars worth of Joseff baubles for decorations!

The first parties saw security guards standing watch so admirers could enjoy but not touch. However, in their drab Brinks-style uniforms, Joan deemed their presence too austere, so every December thereafter she imaginatively changed the apparel of these "guardians of the jewels." One year a guard dressed as a Nubian prince stood beside a stately topiary tree. Another year the jeweled masterpiece was overseen by a dignified gentleman attired as a regal British Beefeater.

The ever-changing elegance of the "Christmas tree to top all Christmas trees" may have been the best of it, but the impeccable planning that went into the entire evening made it year after year an "affair to remember." The unique decor and innovative entertainment—one time provided by strolling minstrels, another by a renowned boys' choir—were incentive enough for those lucky enough to garner an invitation.

The theme always revolved around a single color scheme, which added to the breathtaking ambiance. On one occasion, Joan even dyed her then reddish hair a head-turning blue to match her gown! That Jeff occupied a special place in her heart was obvious. Photos of these parties show him proudly by her side. The cover of the *Los Angeles Times* family section in December 1959 featured young Jeff, then in seventh grade at military school, admiring the resplendent tree and looking equally resplendent in his military uniform.

On a less grand scale, JC's Christmas cards were "show stoppers," too. A December 1956 article in the *Hollywood Citizens News* describing celebrity Christmas cards had this to say about JC's. "The most expensive and ornate card, 5½ by 7½, came from Joan Castle Joseff...plum-colored, the Silver Chalice, measuring five inches, superimposed in silver....Many who saw the card declared it the most breathtaking in their experience."

Besides loving mother, brilliant businesswoman and party giver par excellence, there is yet another, highly important and personally rewarding facet to Joan Castle Joseff's extraordinary personality. She has given untiringly of her time to many civic and charitable organizations, including years of service to the American Cancer Society, WAIF, Toys for Tots, Burbank Hospital, and the John Tracy Clinic for the Deaf (founded by Spencer Tracy).

She has served as secretary of the Advertising Club of Los Angeles. In 1955, the Executive Business Men's Club of New York named her "the world's most glamorous business executive," and shortly thereafter she was the subject of an article in *Fortune* magazine. The following year she was awarded an honorary life membership in the Women of the Motion Picture Industry. Others so honored have included Mary Pickford, Joan Crawford, Dorothy Lamour, and designer Edith Head. On the lighter side, her membership in the Women of America organization once resulted in a charitable fashion show that featured a parade of models wearing Joseff creations, but with a unique "twist" from the *standard* runway fare. These "models" were "five four-legged, champion dogs of the West"!

One of JC's biggest challenges came in 1958 when she was commissioned to design a shrine to Our Lady of Perpetual Help in Van Nuys, California. She studied Byzantine art both in the United States and abroad, and took Jeff with her on a trip to Greece, Yugoslavia and Russia where, in the Joseff tradition, she carefully compiled historical background for her newly-commissioned work. The research served her well. Upon completion, the shrine embodied the

Byzantine tradition and was beautiful to behold, with renderings that included dazzling jewels intricately set to resemble ancient mosaics.

Except when traveling on business or on behalf of her extensive outside interests—she is a Republican National Committeewoman from California, which continues to occupy much of her time and takes her on jaunts throughout the United States and to the inner sanctum of the White House's Oval Office—Joan faithfully arrives at her desk early each morning, just as she has done for many decades. She oversees and controls the logistics involved in the ongoing production of airplane parts, which is now the mainstay of the Joseff operation.

Although distribution of Joseff retail jewelry had been drastically reduced by the late 1960s, a supply of some of the old findings from the "early days" are still being assembled on a very limited basis into finished pieces. Joseff-Hollywood "gems" continue to be in demand for use in films and television programs, and for personal clients to wear at glittering events like the Academy Awards—where JC claims she finds the jewelry more familiar than the faces!

Although the crux of the business now revolves around the foundry operation, this does not supersede Joan's personal commitment to keeping the memory and appreciation of Joseff jewelry alive and well. The business remains a "family affair," just like it was in the early days, when both Eugene's and Joan's mothers also worked for the company. Jeff is now vice-president of sales and his wife Tina is Joan's assistant and dependable "right hand."

Joan Castle Joseff never remarried. She says she "came close" on a few occasions, but knew in her heart that something was missing, which was probably no real surprise. For there are certain special relationships that continue to flourish, even when one partner is not physically present. The magical union of Joan Castle and Eugene Joseff is surely one of them!

Bronze, pearls, crosses, fleur de lis and beautiful stones combine to form a magnificent crown, an unidentified movie piece, probably used numerous times.

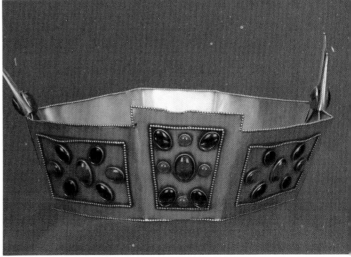

Red and green cabochons adorn a crown designed for *Richard III* (1956). The film's all-star cast included Sir Lawrence Olivier, John Gielgud, and Claire Bloom.

Starlet Joan Leslie surrounded by Joseff jewelry. Don't stand up Joan!

Future president Ronald Reagan, shown here in 1950 placing crown later to be worn by Miss California on the head of actress Ann Blyth.

Claire Trevor glows and glitters in jewels by Joseff for 1952's *Stop, You're Killing Me*, a Damon Runyon yarn that also starred tough guy Broderick Crawford.

Deborah Kerr, whose career in the United States was just starting, posed for this publicity shot in 1949, wearing a Joseff necklace. She had already appeared opposite Clark Gable in *The Hucksters* and Walter Pidgeon in *If Winter Comes*.

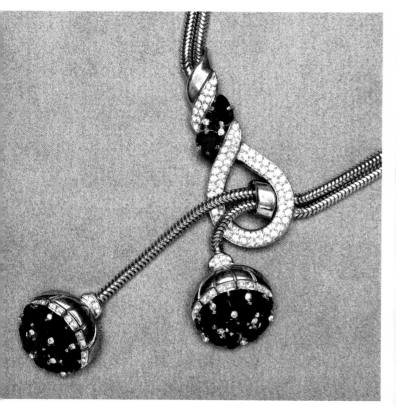

This necklace of faux sapphires and diamonds, worn by Larraine Day in *I Married a Communist* (1949), has an unusual and particularly graceful design.

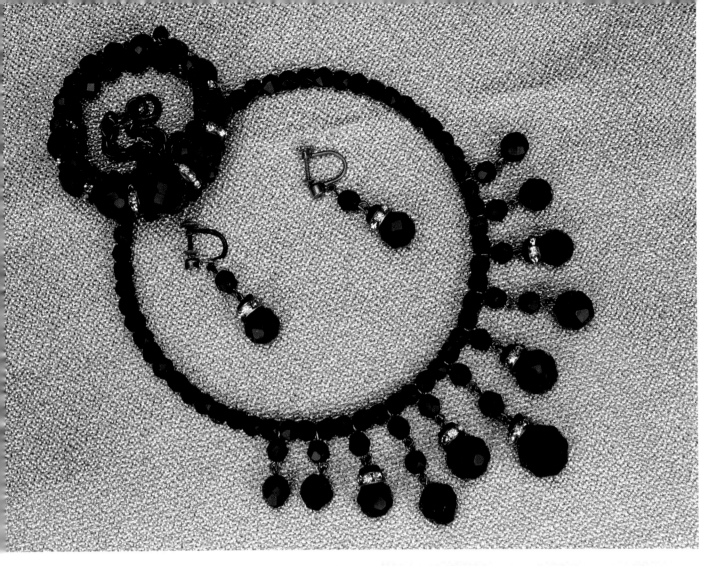

These French jet pieces were aptly designed to be worn by Elsa Lanchester in *Frenchie,* a 1950 film that followed the story line of *Destry Rides Again.* Lanchester played a gambling tutor and companion of Shelley Winters.

167

Bette Davis and her daughter's fiance, Richard Anderson, in a scene from *The Story of a Divorce.*

An auspicious line-up! Top to bottom: an emerald and diamond brooch from *Lillian Russell* (1940); of more recent vintage, an emerald drop necklace worn by Brenda Vaccaro in a 1990 episode of *Murder She Wrote;* again from *Lillian Russell* a pear-shaped emerald and diamond necklace worn by Alice Faye; and last, but certainly not least, another emerald and diamond "knockout," this one with three tassel drops, worn by Marie Windsor in *Frenchie* (1950).

Judy Holliday certainly *wasn't Born Yesterday.* She snared this beautiful emerald and diamond beauty from mogul Broderick Crawford, in the 1950 film of the same title! The emerald bracelet and brooch at left appeared on the late Irene Dunne in *Love Affair* (1939).

This sparkling duo, consisting of an emerald and diamond necklace with matching bracelet, was first seen on Anita Louise in *The Fighting Guardsman* (1945). They recently dazzled our eyes again in the 1990 TV miniseries *People Like Us.*

169

Ava Gardner in a scene from *The Great Sinner*, also starring Gregory Peck. Necklace at top in photo above was also worn by her in the film.

170

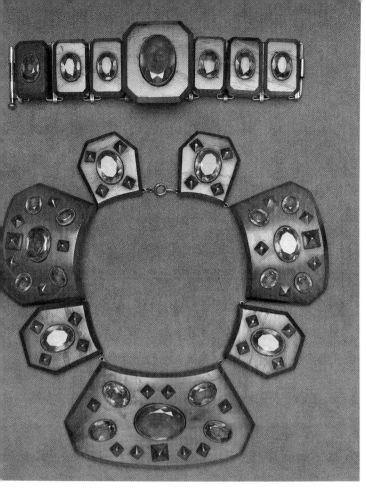

Rosalind Russell sports the bold Joseff necklace of wood inset with gold and semi-precious stones for her role in *Woman of Distinction* (1950).

Here's Kay Francis wearing the same necklace, and matching bracelet, ten years earlier in 1940's *It's a Date*, starring Deanna Durbin.

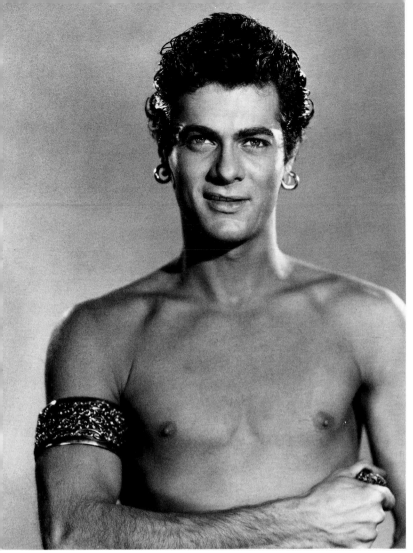

Here's Tony Curtis, complete with arm bracelet and earrings for his role in *The Prince Who Was a Thief*. Universal called it "up the ladder of fame" for this ex-New Yorker—and stated he could thank his fans for the biggest break handed a newcomer in Hollywood. Curtis is pictured at right with his co-star Piper Laurie.

Double duty for these dynamic cuffs! They were first worn by Yvonne DeCarlo in 1948's *Casbah* and three years later by Tony Curtis in *The Prince Who Was a Thief*.

These pieces are from *Little Egypt*, the 1951 film starring Rhonda Fleming and Mark Stevens.

Rhonda Fleming, decked out in all her finery, goes over script between takes of *Little Egypt*.

This unusual headpiece was also worn by Rhonda Fleming in *Little Egypt*. The choker encircled Shirley MacLaine's neck in *Around the World in Eighty Days* five years later, a movie which revealed lush technicolor, refinements on the previous Cinerama and Todd-AO techniques, along with a revolutionary six channel sound system.

This swirling double pearl and rhinestone brooch,
and the elaborate necklace at right, helped to make
Ginger Rogers a "Dreamboat" in 1953's film by the
same name.

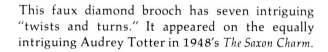

This faux diamond brooch has seven intriguing "twists and turns." It appeared on the equally intriguing Audrey Totter in 1948's *The Saxon Charm*.

1956 saw these on the dainty ears of the future Princess of Monaco, Grace Kelly, when she starred with Bing Crosby and Frank Sinatra in *High Society*, a remake of the classic *Philadelphia Story*. The design was later converted into the Joseff retail line, with much success.

As Montgomery Clift learned at the film's conclusion, this beautiful necklace of pearls and crystals was well-suited to the deceptively fragile delicacy of Olivia deHavilland in *The Heiress* (1952).

Necklace and earrings worn by Rita Hayworth in *Salome*.

In 1938, *Alexander's Ragtime Band* broke a nine-year attendance record at New York's Roxy Theatre, and drew the largest crowd ever to purchase opening day tickets.

This elaborate antique-finished five-piece parure was worn by the always imposing Dame Judith Anderson in 1953's *Salome* with Rita Hayworth and Stewart Granger.

179

The *Salome* necklaces and other jewels are shown in this scene from the film. Charles Laughton is as resplendent in his gold bib as the matching one in a slightly different style that he's placing around Rita Hayworth's neck. Also note the elaborate belt.

Ann Sothern, whose daughter Tisha Sterling followed in her mother's footsteps, is dazzling in these jewels by Joseff for her role in the 1949 musical *Nancy Goes to Rio*. The film also starred Jane Powell and a permanent fixture in any film with Latin overtones—Carmen Miranda.

Another unbelievable necklace! This one for Carmen Miranda to wear in *Nancy Goes to Rio*.

Belting out a song in *Call Me Madam* was second-nature for its star Ethel Merman. Creating this gorgeous necklace was also second-nature for the Joseff team.

Fabulous jewelry for a fabulous movie—*Some Like It Hot*—and its equally fabulous leading lady—Marilyn Monroe! The 1959 comedy also starred Jack Lemmon and Tony Curtis.

A large yet delicately filigreed cross pendant is flanked by equally feminine earrings accented with brilliant ruby red stones. Both were worn by Lucille Ball in *Auntie Mame* (1958).

A massive belt for a tiny waist, this was worn by Dyan Cannon in 1971's *The Love Machine*.

Scarabs and snakes ornament this lariat belt and accompanying bracelets, worn by Elizabeth Taylor in *Cleopatra* (1963).

The asp belt worn by Elizabeth Taylor in *Cleopatra*.

TV crowns. On left, worn by Elizabeth Taylor in "Malice in Wonderland," the story of the infamous feud between Hedda Hopper and Louella Parsons. On right, an elaborate beauty featured in the "Batman" series.

1989's "Elvis and Me" was a short-lived television series. These rings were made by Joseff-Hollywood to represent the gigantic aquamarine worn decades ago by Elvis (left), and Priscilla Presley's original engagement ring (right).

More television and movie crowns, including a petaled hairpiece. The pearl crown on right was worn by Joan Collins in the "Dynasty" television series.

Epilogue

According to the director of the American Film Institute National Center for Film and Video Presentation, "…most of the 150,600,000 feet of crumbling nitrate-based film in their possession must be transferred to acetate stock by the year 2010 or be lost forever. The cost would be $200 million."[1]

Every enterprise has its unsung heroes, and the film industry is no exception. The early pioneers—many of whom have long since been forgotten by all but true film buffs—made it happen. But without those dedicated folks behind the scenes who breathe life and authenticity into the movies…costume designers, art directors, set designers, music directors and choreographers, to mention just a few…the industry probably would have faltered and died long before Cecil B. DeMille had a chance to hop that train for Flagstaff!

Eugene Joseff contributed mightily to this scenario, designing and executing jewelry for well over ninety percent of the movies from those shining decades of the 1930s and 1940s. Comedic errors may have, from time to time, crept into the final product in other areas of film-making, but one thing is certain. When called for, the jewelry Eugene Joseff provided was historically accurate and always beautiful to behold. In his fourteen, tragically short years in the industry his contribution to the ambiance of the movies was astounding and monumental.

The studios, outside enterprises, and all those individuals who remember—and continue to enjoy—this unique part of our history, have a vested responsibility to the men and women both in front of and behind the cameras who poured their talents into creating these entertainment masterpieces. They are a uniquely innovative slice of America's cultural heritage, and each film is a gem to be treasured. Just as Joan Castle Joseff has treasured those other "gems"—the ones Joseff of Hollywood made a part of movie history.

Notes

Scene I. Movies—The Beginning
1. Richard Griffith and Arthur Mayer, *The Movies*, 3.
2. Ibid., 97.
3. Jesse L. Lasky, Jr., *Whatever Happened to Hollywood?*, 2.
4. Ibid., 6.
5. Ibid., 7.
6. John Kobal, *Gods and Goddesses of the Movies*, 147.

Scene II. Enter Eugene Joseff
1. Samuel Marx, *Mayer and Thalberg, The Make-Believe Saints*, 83.
2. George MacDonald Fraser, *The Hollywood History of the World*, xiv.
3. George Amberg, *The New York Times Film Reviews*, 165.
4. John Kobal, *Gods and Goddess of the Movies*, 78.
5. John Kobal, *Gods and Goddesses of the Movies*, 117.

Scene III. Enter Joan Castle
1. Jesse L. Lasky, Jr., *Whatever Happened to Hollywood?*, 277.

Scene IV. Movies—The Golden Years
1. George MacDonald Fraser, *The Hollywood History of the World*, xix.
2. James Watters, *Return Engagement, Faces to Remember—Then and Now*, 7.
3. Paul Trent, *Those Fabulous Movie Years: The 1930s*, 69.

Scene V. "Gone With The Wind"
1. Herb Bridges and Terryl C. Bookman, *Gone With The Wind, The Definitive Illustrated History of the Book, the Movie, and the Legend*, 5.
2. "Suzy," *The New York Post*, July 26, 1990.
3. Herb Bridges and Terryl C. Bookman, *Gone With The Wind, The Definitive Illustrated History of the Book, the Movie, and the Legend*, 16.
4. Jesse L. Lasky, Jr., *Whatever Happened to Hollywood?*, 229.
5. George Amberg, *The New York Times Film Reviews, 1913-1970*, 185.
6. Herb Bridges and Terryl C. Bookman, *Gone With The Wind, The Definitive Illustrated History of the Book, the Movie, and the Legend*, 174.

Epilogue
1. "Closing the Dream Factory," *California Magazine*, December, 1989.

Bibliography

Amberg, George. *The New York Times Film Reviews, 1913-1970*. New York: Arno Press, in cooperation with Quadrangle Books, Inc., 1971.

Blum, Daniel. *New Pictorial History of the Talkies*, New York: G.P. Putnam's Sons, 1958.

Bridges, Herb, and Terryl C. Boodman. *Gone With the Wind, The Definitive Illustrated History of the Book, the Movie, and the Legend*. New York: Simon and Schuster, 1989.

California Magazine. Los Angeles: California Magazines Partnership, December 1989.

Finler, Joel. *All-Time Movie Favorites*. Rowayton, Connecticut: Longmeadow Press, 1975.

Fraser, George MacDonald. *The Hollywood History of the World*. New York: William Morrow, 1988.

Griffith, Richard, and Arthur Mayer. *The Movies*. New York: Simon and Schuster, 1957, revised 1970.

Kobal, John. *Gods and Goddesses of the Movies*. New York: Crescent Books, 1963.

Lasky, Jesse L., Jr. *Whatever Happened to Hollywood?* New York: Funk and Wagnalls, 1973.

Maltin, Leonard. *TV Movies and Video Guide*, 1990, New York: New American Library, 1989.

Martin, Mick and Porter, Marsha, *Video Movie Guide*, 1989, New York: Ballentine Books, 1988.

Marx, Samuel. *Mayer and Thalberg, The Make-Believe Saints*. New York: Random House, 1975.

"Movie Show," February 1948.

"Suzy." *The New York Post*, July 26, 1990.

Trent, Paul. *Those Fabulous Movie Years: The 1930s*. Barre, Massachusetts: Barre Publishing, 1975. Distributed by Crown, New York.

Watters, James. *Return Engagement, Faces to Remember—Then and Now*. New York: Clarkson N. Potter, Inc., 1984. Distributed by Crown, New York.

Wilkerson, Tichi and Marcia Borie. *The Hollywood Reporter*. New York: Coward-McCann, Inc., 1984.

Movies . . . Movies . . . Movies . . .

Joan Castle Joseff estimates that Joseff jewelry and props appeared in films and television programs numbering in the thousands. On that awesome note, the following is but a very partial list. In some instances, the date shown may represent the year the assignment was completed and not the year the movie was released. In others, working titles may later have been changed and, therefore, dates and final titles could not be determined.

Abbott and Costello Go to Mars (1947)
Above Suspicion (1943)
Ada (1961)
Adam's Rib (1949)
Adventure in Diamonds (1940)
Adventures of Don Juan, The (1949)
Adventures of Mark Twain, The (1944)
Affair in Trinidad (1952)
Against All Flags (1952)
Air Cadet (1951)
Airport '75 (1974)
Algiers (1938)
All About Eve (1950)
All Fall Down (1962)
All I Desire (1953)
All the King's Men (1949)
All This and Heaven Too (1937)
Americanization of Emily, The (1964)
Always Goodbye (1938)
Anchors Aweigh (1945)
An American in Paris (1951)
Androcles and the Lion (1952)
Angel Face (1952)
Angel from Texas, An (1940)
Angels with Dirty Faces (1937)
Anna and the King of Siam (1946)
Annabel Takes a Tour (1938)
Anna Karenina (1935)
Annie Get Your Gun (1950)
Anthony Adverse (1936)
Anything Can Happen (1952)
Anything Goes (1936)
April in Paris (1952)
Arch of Triumph (1948)
Army Brat (1947)
Arnelo Affair, The (1947)
Around the World in 80 Days (1956)
Arrow in the Dust (1954)
Arsenic and Old Lace (1943)
Art of Love, The (1965)
Asphalt Jungle, The (1950)
Atlantis, The Lost Continent (1961)
At Sword's Point (1951)
Auntie Mame (1958)

Baby Doll (1956)
Bachelor in Paradise (1961)
Bad and the Beautiful, The (1952)
Bagdad (1945)
Bahama Passage (1941)
Balalaika (1939)
Band of Angels, A (1957)
Band Wagon, The (1953)
Barkleys of Broadway, The (1949)
Barretts of Wimpole Street, The (1956)
Batteries Not Included (1987)
Beau Geste (1939)
Bedtime for Bonzo (1951)

Bedtime Story (1941)
Belle of New York, The (1952)
Ben Hur (1959)
Best Years of our Lives, The (1946)
Between Two Worlds (1944)
Big Country, The (1958)
Big Sleep, The (1946)
Big Town (1947)
Big Trees, The (1952)
Birds and the Bees, The (1947)
Birth of the Blues (1941)
Blackboard Jungle, The (1954)
Black Magic (1949)
Blind Alibi (1938)
Blood Brothers (1977)
Blow Up (1967)
Blue Gardenia, The (1953)
Blue Veil, The (1951)
Body Disappears, The (1941)
Boom Town (1940)
Born Yesterday (1950)
Brave Bulls, The (1950)
Breakfast at Tiffany's (1961)
Breaking the Ice (1974)
Bribe, The (1949)
Bride Came COD, The (1941)
Bride Comes Home, The (1935)
Brigadoon (1954)
Broadway Melody of 1936 (1936)
Broadway Melody of 1940 (1940)
Bronco Squad (1950)
Brothers Karamazov, The (1958)
Buccaneer, The (1958)
Buccaneer's Girl (1950)
Bullwhipped (1958)
By the Light of the Silvery Moon (1953)

Cafe Society (1938)
Calcutta (1945)
Call it a Day (1937)
Call Me Madam (1952)
Comanche Territory (1949)
Camelot (1967)
Camille (1937)
Can Can (1960)
Captain Black Jack (1952)
Captain Blood (1935)
Captain Horatio Hornblower (1951)
Carpetbaggers, The (1964)
Carriage Entrance (1949)
Casablanca (1942)
Casbah (1947)
Cass Timberlane (1947)
Cat and the Canary, The (1939)
Cat on a Hot Tin Roof (1958)
Catered Affair, The (1956)
Cattle King (1963)
Centennial Summer (1946)

Charlie's Aunt (1951)
Chat Talk
Cheap Detective, The (1978)
Cheyenne (1947)
China (1943)
China Seas (1935)
Chinatown (1973)
Christmas in Connecticut (1945)
City Beneath the Sea (1953)
City Confidential (1952)
Cleopatra (1963)
Close to My Heart (1951)
Clown, The (1952)
Cluny Brown (1946)
Cockeyed Miracle, The (1946)
Come Be My Love (1946)
Come Live With Me (1940)
Conquest (1937)
Constant Nymph, The (1943)
Commanche Territory (1950)
Coral Browne (1958)
Count of Monte Cristo, The (1934)
Country Girl, The (1954)
Country Music Holiday (1958)
Cousin Tundifer (1962)
Crack Up (1936)
Critic's Choice (1963)
Cry Havoc (1943)
Crystal Ball, The (1943)
Cynthia (1947)

Dakota (1945)
Dancing With Tears (1946)
Dangerous When Wet (1952)
Danger Street
Dangerous Partners (1945)
Dangerous to Know (1938)
Danger Signal (1945)
Dark Corner, The (1946)
Dark Mirror, The (1946)
Dark Victory (1937)
Darling Lili (1970)
Date With Judy, A (1948)
Death in the Doll House (1949)
Desert Hawk, The (1950)
Desert Song, The (1953)
Design for Scandal (1941)
Designing Woman (1957)
Desire (1936)
Desire Under the Elms (1958)
Detective Story (1951)
Devotion (1946)
Dial M for Murder (1954)
Diamond Jim (1950)
Diamond Queen, The (1953)
Diane (1955)
Dinner at Eight (1933)
Divorce (1945)

Dodge City (1947)
Doll Face (1945)
Dolly Madison
Dolly Sisters, The (1945)
Don Renegade (1951)
Don't Answer the Phone (1980)
Double Feature (1977)
Double Indemnity (1944)
Double Life, A (1947)
Double Take (1949)
Down to Earth (1947)
Do You Love Me? (1946)
Dragonwyck (1946)
Dreamboat (1952)
Dream Wife (1953)
DuBarry was a Lady (1943)
Duchess of Idaho (1950)
Duel in the Sun (1946)

Eagle and the Hawk, The (1950)
Easter Parade (1949)
East of Sumatra (1953)
Easy to Wed (1947)
Emperor Waltz, The (1948)
Enchanted Cottage, The (1945)
Ever Since Eve (1937)
Everybody's Old Man (1930s)
Executive Suite (1954)

Face in the Crowd, A (1957)
Family, The (1976)
Family Next Door, The
Fan, The (1949)
Farmer's Daughter, The (1947)
Fastest Gun Alive, The (1956)
Father of the Bride (1950)
Faulty Row (1947)
Female Animal, The (1957)
Fighting Guardsman, The (1947)
First Traveling Saleslady, The (1956)
Flame and the Flesh (1954)
Flamingo Road (1949)
Flaxy Martin (1949)
Flim Flam Man, The (1966)
Flower Drum Song (1961)
Follow the Boys (1963)
Fools for Scandal (1938)
Forever Amber (1947)
Forever Female (1953)
Forever My Love (1962)
For Me and My Gal (1942)
For Those Who Dare (1947)
Fortunes of Captain Blood (1950)
For Whom the Bell Tolls (1943)
Four Horsemen of the Apocalypse (1961)
Four Wives (1939)
Franz Liszt Story, The
Frenchie (1950)

Frenchman's Creek (1944)
From Here to Eternity (1953)
From This Day Forward (1946)
Frontier Doctor (1957)
Fuller Brush Girl, The (1950)

Gallant Blade, The (1948)
Gaslight (1949)
Gay Senorita, The (1949)
Gemini (1976)
Gentlemen's Agreement (1947)
Gentlemen Prefer Blondes (1953)
Giant (1956)
Gibson Girl, The (1949)
Gigi (1958)
Gilda (1946)
Girl From Jones Beach, The (1949)
Girl Who Had Everything, The (1953)
Glass Key, The (1942)
Global Affair, A (1963)
Godfather, The (1972)
Golden Arrow (1936)
Golden Earrings (1947)
Golden Hawk, The (1952)
Golden Horde, The (1951)
Gold is Where You Find It (1938)
Good Earth, The (1936)
Gone with the Wind (1939)
Goodbye, Mr. Chips (1939)
Goodbye My Fancy (1951)
Go West Young Man (1936)
Golden Earring (1947)
Great Caruso, The (1951)
Greatest, The (1976)
Greatest Show on Earth, The (1952)
Great Gambini, The (1937)
Great Gatsby, The (1949)
Great Jewel Robber, The (1950)
Great Lover, The (1949)
Great Man's Lady, The (1942)
Great Sinner, The (1949)
Great Waltz, The (1938)
Great Ziegfield, The (1936)
Green Dolphin Street (1947)
Green Mansions (1959)
Green Years, The (1946)
Guy, A Girl and A Gob, A (1940)
Guys and Dolls (1955)
Gypsy (1962)
Guilty Bystander (1950)
Gunga Din (1939)

Hanging Tree, The (1958)
Happy Chance Saloon (1946)
Happy Time, The (1952)
Harriet Craig (1950)
Harvey (1950)
Harvey Girls, The (1945)
Havana Rose (1951)
Heaven Can Wait (1977)
Heiress, The (1949)
Helen of Troy (1955)
Hellzapoppin' (1942)
Her Cardboard Lover (1942)
Here Comes the Groom (1951)
Her Highness and the Bellboy (1945)
Her Jungle Love (1938)
Her Kind of Man (1946)
High and the Mighty, The (1954)
High Sierra (1941)
High Society (1956)
His Kind of Woman (1949)
Hitler's Gang (1945)
Hit the Deck (1955)
Hitting a New High (1937)
Hold Back the Dawn (1941)
Holiday (1938)
Holiday for Sinners (1952)
Holiday in Mexico (1949)
Hollywood Canteen (1944)
Hollywood Hotel (1937)
Homestretch, The (1947)
Honky Tonk (1941)
Hoodlum Empire (1952)
Hoodlum Saint, The (1946)
Hot Blood (1956)
Hotel Berlin (1945)
Houdini (1953)

How the West was Won (1962)
How to Marry a Millionaire (1953)
Hucksters, The (1947)
Humoresque (1946)
Hunchback of Notre Dame, The (1939)

If I'm Lucky (1945)
I Love Melvin (1953)
I Married a Woman (1956)
If I Were King (1938)
If Winter Comes (1949)
Illegal (1955)
I'll Take Romance (1937)
Imagination
I Married a Communist (1949)
I Met Him in Paris (1937)
Imperfect Lady, The (1947)
Indiscreet (1958)
In a Lonely Place (1947)
Inside Daisy Clover (1966)
Inside Straight (1951)
International Settlement (1938)
It's A Big Country (1952)
It's a Date (1947)
It's a Wonderful Life (1949)
I've Always Loved You (1946)
I Wanted Wings (1941)

Jack of Diamonds (1967)
Jazz Singer, The (1953)
Jeanne Eagels (1957)
Jezebel (1937)
Joan of Arc (1948)
Johnny Angel (1945)
Johnny Tremain (1957)
Jolsen Sings Again (1949)
Juarez (1939)
Jumbo (1962)
June Bride (1948)
Jungle Book (1942)
Jupiter's Darling (1954)
Just This Once (1951)

Kathleen (1941)
Katie Did It (1951)
Keeper of the Flame (1942)
Killer that Stalked New York, The (1943)
Killing, The (1956)
King & I, The (1956)
King Rat
King Solomon's Mines (1950)
Kings Row (1942)
King's Thief, The (1955)
Kismet (1943)
Kissing Bandit, The (1947)
Kiss Me Kate (1953)
Kiss of Death (1947)
Kitty (1945)
Klondike Annie (1936)

Ladies in Retirement (1941)
Lady and the Knight, The
Lady and the Mob, The (1939)
Lady and the Prowler, The (1957)
Lady Eve, The (1941)
Lady Godiva (1955)
Lady in the Dark (1944)
Lady in the Iron Mask (1952)
Lady in the Lake (1946)
Lady on a Train (1945)
Lady of the Tropics (1939)
Last Hero, The (1947)
Last of Mrs. Cheney, The (1937)
Last Time I Saw Paris, The (1954)
Las Vegas Nights (1941)
Late George Apley, The (1946)
Latin Lovers (1953)
La Traviata (1949)
Law and the Lady, The (1951)
Lawless Valley, The
Law of the Tropics (1941)
Leave Her to Heaven (1945)
Legend of Black Bart, The (1947)
Lemon Drop Kid, The (1951)
Les Girls (1957)
Letter For Evie, A (1945)
Let's Fall in Love (1947)
Let's Live a Little (1948)

Letter from an Unknown Woman (1947)
Libeled Lady (1936)
Life Begins at 8:30 (1942)
Life of Emil Zola, The (1937)
Life With Father (1949)
Lili (1952)
Lillian Russell (1940)
Little Egypt (1951)
Little Foxes, The (1941)
Little Miss Marker (1979)
Little Princess, The (1939)
Little Women (1949)
Lizzie (1957)
Lloyds of London (1936)
Lone Star (1952)
Long Hot Summer, The (1958)
Look for the Silver Lining (1949)
Look Who's Laughing (1941)
Lorna Doone (1950)
Lost Horizon (1937)
Lost Weekend, The (1945)
Louisa (1950)
Love Affair (1939)
Love from a Stranger (1947)
Love I'm After, The (1937)
Love Laughs at Andy Hardy (1946)
Love Machine, The (1971)
Love Me or Leave Me (1956)
Loved One, The (1965)
Lovely to Look At (1952)
Loves of Carmen, The (1947)
Louisa (1950)
Lucky Jordan (1942)
Lucky Me (1953)
Lulu Belle (1948)

Macbeth (1948)
Macao (1952)
Madame Bovary (1949)
Madame Curie (1943)
Madame X (1966)
Mad Miss Manton, The (1938)
Magnificent Doll (1946)
Magnificent Fraud, The (1953)
Magnificent Yankees, The (1950)
Maisie (1939)
Maisie Goes to Reno (1944)
Maltese Falcon, The (1941)
Mame (1973)
Man Alive (1945)
Mandingo (1974)
Man I Love, The (1946)
Man of Conquest (1939)
Mannequin (1937)
Man Who Came to Dinner, The (1942)
Man With a Cloak, The (1951)
Margie (1946)
Marie Antoinette (1938)
Marjorie Morningstar (1958)
Marked Woman (1937)
Mark of the Avenger (1950)
Marriage is a Private Affair (1944)
Maru Maru (1952)
Mary of Scotland (1936)
Mary Queen of Scots (1971)
Mask of Demetrius, The (1944)
Mask of the Avenger (1951)
Masquerade in Mexico (1945)
Maverick Queen (1955)
Maytime (1937)
Meet Me in Las Vegas (1955)
Meet Me in St. Louis (1944)
Memory of Love (1947)
Merry Widow, The (1952)
Merton of the Movies (1947)
Mexicana (1946)
Mexican Hayride (1948)
Midnight Kiss, The (1949)
Mildred Pierce (1945)
Milleroon Caoe, The
Million Dollar Baby (1941)
Million Dollar Legs (1939)
Million Dollar Mermaid (1952)
Miracle in the Rain (1956)
Miss Susie Slagle's (1945)
Mogambo (1953)
Monkey Business (1952)
Monsieur Beaucaire (1946)

Montana Bell (1952)
Moonlight Ray (1951)
Moss Rose (1947)
Most Wanted (1976)
Mourning Becomes Electra (1947)
Mr. and Mrs. North (1941)
Mr. Imperium (1951)
Mr. Peabody & the Mermaid (1948)
Mr. Skeffington (1944)
Mrs. Miniver (1942)
Mrs. Parkington (1944)
Murder at the Gallup (1963)
Murder by Death (1975)
Murder on the Orient Express (1974)
Mutiny (1952)
My Cousin Rachel (1953)
My Darling Clementine (1946)
My Dream is Yours (1949)
My Fair Lady (1964)
My Gun is Quick (1957)
My Little Chickadee (1940)
My Love, Come Back (1947)
Mystery Street (1950)
My Tutor (1983)
My Wild Irish Rose (1953)

Nancy Drew and the Hidden Staircase (1937)
Nancy Goes to Rio (1949)
National Velvet (1944)
Naughty Marietta (1935)
Neptune's Daughter (1949)
Never So Few (1959)
Never Wave at a WAC (1953)
New Moon (1940)
New York, New York (1976)
Nice Girl (1941)
Night and Day (1946)
Nightmare Alley (1947)
Night Must Fall (1937)
Night of the Iguana (1964)
Night of the Quarter Moon (1958)
Ninotchka (1939)
Nob Hill (1945)
Nobody Lives Forever (1946)
Nocturne (1946)
North by Northwest (1959)
No Questions Asked (1951)
Northwest Outpost (1947)
Not for Hire (1960)
Notorious (1946)
Now Voyager (1942)
Nurse's Secret, The (1941)

Of Human Bondage (1944)
Oklahoma Kid (1939)
Old Acquaintance (1943)
Old Maid, The (1937)
Once Upon a Honeymoon (1948)
One More Tomorrow (1946)
One of our Spies is Missing (1966)
One Rich Dowager (1947)
One Touch of Venus (1948)
On the Town (1948)
Our Hearts Were Young and Gay (1944)
Our Miss Brooks (1956)
Our Neighbors, the Carters (1939)

Pajama Game, The (1957)
Paleface, The (1948)
Paradine Case, The (1947)
Pardon My Past (1945)
Paris Underground (1945)
Party Girl, The (1958)
Payment on Demand (1951)
Peking Express (1951)
Penelope (1966)
People are Funny (1946)
Perfect Marriage, The (1946)
Perfect Strangers (1950)
Petersville Diamond, The (1942)
Petty Girl, The (1950)
Peyton Place (1957)
Philadelphia Story, The (1940)
Picture of Dorian Gray (1946)
Pirate, The (1948)
Pirates of Monterey (1944)
Pittsburgh (1942)

Place in the Sun, A (1951)
Please Don't Eat the Daisies (1960)
Pleasure Palace, The (1980)
Pollyanna (1960)
Possessed (1947)
Postman Always Rings Twice, The (1946)
Pot O' Gold (1941)
Price of Fear, The (1956)
Prince and the Showgirl, The (1956)
Prince of Foxes, The (1948)
Prince and the Pauper, The (1937)
Prince Who was a Thief, The (1950)
Prisoner of Zenda, The (1937)
Private Lives of Elizabeth & Essex, The (1939)
Private Secretary (1935)
Prize, The (1963)
Prodigal, The (1955)
Psycho (1960)

Quo Vadis (1951)

Racket, The (1951)
Rage in Heaven, A (1941)
Rains Came, The (1939)
Rains of Ranchipur (1955)
Raintree County (1957)
Random Harvest (1942)
Reap the Wild Wind (1942)
Rear Window (1954)
Rebecca (1940)
Rebel Without a Cause (1955)
Red Planet Mars (1952)
Relentless (1942)
Remember the Night (1940)
Return of Monte Cristo, The (1948)
Return to King Solomon's Mines (1950)
Rhapsody (1954)
Richard III (1956)
Rich, Young and Pretty (1950)
Ride the Pink Horse (1949)
Rio Rita (1942)
River Lady (1948)
Road to Morocco, The (1942)
Road to Rio, The (1947)
Rogues of Sherwood Forest (1950)
Romance of Rosy Ridge, The (1949)
Roman Holiday (1953)
Romeo & Juliet (1936)
Rosalie (1937)
Rose Marie (1936)
Rosemary's Baby (1968)
Royal Scandal, A (1945)
Royal Wedding (1950)

Sabrina (1954)
Sainted Sisters, The (1948)
Sally and Saint Anne (1952)
Salome (1950)
Samson & Delilah (1949)
Sand (1949)
Sandpiper, The (1965)
Saratoga (1937)
Saratoga Trunk (1949)
Saxon Charm, The (1948)
Say It in French (1950)
Scandal in Paris, A (1946)
Scaramouche (1952)
Scared Stiff (1953)
Scarlet Angel (1952)
Sea Chase, The (1955)
Sea Hawk, The (1940)
Sea of Grass, The (1947)
Secret Heart (1946)
Second Shot, The (1949)
Secret Beyond the Door (1950)
Secrets of an Actress (1937)
Sentimental Journey (1946)
September Affair, (1950)

Sergeant York (1941)
Service Deluxe (1949)
Seven Brides for Seven Brothers (1954)
Seven Thieves (1959)
Seventh Sin, The (1957)
Seven Year Itch, The (1955)
Shadow in the Sky (1951)
Shadow of a Woman (1946)
Shaft (1971)
Shakedown (1950)
Shanghai Express (1932)
Shanghai Gesture (1949)
She (1935)
She Done Him Wrong (1933)
Sheriff of Fractured Jaw (1958)
She's Back on Broadway (1953)
She's No Lady (1937)
She's Working Her Way Through College (1952)
Shine on Harvest Moon (1943)
Showboat (1951)
Silk Stockings (1957)
Silver Chalice, The (1954)
Sinbad the Sailor (1950)
Sincerely Yours (1955)
Since You Went Away (1947)
Sincerely Yours (1955)
Singing in the Rain (1952)
Singing Nun, The (1966)
Sink the Bismarck (1960)
Siren of Atlantis (1948)
Sirocco (1951)
Sir Walter Raleigh
Sisters, The (1949)
Skirts Ahoy (1952)
Small Town Girl (1936)
Smart Girl (1935)
Smash Up (1947)
So Big (1953)
So Evil My Love (1948)
Somebody Loves Me (1952)
Some Like it Hot (1959)
Song of the Thin Man (1947)
Sons of the Musketeers (1949)
Song Without End (1960)
Sorry Wrong Number (1948)
So This is Love (1953)
South of St. Louis (1949)
South Sea Siren (1947)
Spaceballs (1987)
Spartacus (1960)
Spellbinder, The (1939)
Spider, The (1945)
Splendor in the Grass (1961)
Stage Door (1937)
Stage Fright (1950)
Star is Born, A (1936)
Star is Born, A (1954)
Stolen Heaven (1938)
Stolen Holiday (1930s)
Stop, You're Killing Me (1952)
Story of Three Loves, The (1953)
Stork Club, The (1945)
Storm Warning (1951)
Story of Monty Stratton, The (1947)
Storm Warning (1949)
Story of a Divorce, The (1947)
Strange Door, The (1951)
Strange Journey, The (1946)
Strange Lady in Town (1955)
Stranger, The (1946)
Stranger Wore a Gun, The (1952)
Strawberry Blonde, The (1941)
Streetcar Named Desire, A (1951)
Strictly Dishonourable (1951)
Student Tour (1934)
Suez (1938)
Sullivan's Travels (1941)
Summer Holiday (1947)
Summer Place (1959)

Sunbonnet Sue (1945)
Sunday in New York (1963)
Sunset Boulevard (1950)
Susan and God (1940)
Suspense (1946)
Suspicion (1941)
Swan, The (1956)
Sweet Bird of Youth (1962)

Take a Letter Darling (1942)
Take Me Out to the Ballgame (1951)
Talk About a Lady (1946)
Talk of the Town (1949)
Tars and Spars (1946)
Taras Bulba (1962)
Tea and Sympathy (1956)
Tea for Two (1950)
Teacher's Pet (1958)
Teahouse of the August Moon (1956)
Tell It to the Judge (1951)
Ten Commandments, The (1956)
Ten North Frederick (1958)
Ten Tall Men (1951)
Tenth Avenue Angel (1948)
Ten Thousand Bedrooms (1956)
Test Pilot (1938)
Texas (1941)
Texas Lady (1955)
Thank Your Lucky Stars (1943)
That Certain Feeling (1956)
That Certain Woman (1937)
That Forsyte Woman (1949)
That Hamilton Woman (1941)
That Night in Rio (1941)
That Touch of Mink (1962)
There Goes My Heart (1938)
They Drive by Night (1940)
They Met in Bombay (1941)
They Won't Believe Me (1947)
Thief, A (1955)
Thief of Baghdad, The (1940)
Thief of Baghdad, The (1960)
Thin Man Goes Home, The (1939)
Thief Who Came to Dinner, The (1973)
Thirty-Nine Steps, The (1935)
This Gun for HIre (1942)
This Time for Keeps (1939)
This Woman is Dangerous (1952)
Those Redheads from Seattle (1953)
Thousand and One Nights, A (1939)
Thousands Cheer (1943)
Three Darling Daughters (1948)
Three for Bedroom C (1951)
Three for the Show (1939)
Three Hearts for Julia (1942)
Three Little Girls in Blue (1946)
Three Little Words (1950)
Three Loves has Nancy (1938)
Three Musketeers, The (1939)
Three Musketeers, The (1948)
Thrill of a Romance (1945)
Thunder in the Sun (1959)
Thunder on the Hill (1951)
Till the Clouds Roll By (1946)
Time after Time (1978)
Time out of Mind (1947)
Time to Kill (1947)
To Catch a Thief (1955)
To Each His Own (1946)
To Have and Have Not (1945)
To Please A Lady (1950)
Toast of New Orleans, The (1950)
Tokyo Rose (1945)
Too Hot to Handle (1958)
Tom, Dick and Harry (1940)
Topper Takes a Trip (1939)
Torch Song (1953)
Tower of London (1939)
Trespass (1974)
True Confession (1937)

True Grit (1969)
Tunnel of Love (1958)
Two Faced Woman (1941)
Two Mrs. Carrolls, The (1946)
Two Sisters from Boston (1946)
2001: A Space Odyssey (1968)
Two Tickets to Broadway (1951)
Tycoon, The (1947)

Undercover Maisie (1947)
Undercurrent (1946)
Unfaithful, The (1947)
Unfinished Dance, The (1947)
Unsinkable Molly Brown, The (1964)
Untamed Frontier (1952)
Up in Central Park (1948)

Valentino (1951)
Valley of Decision, The (1945)
Valley of the Kings (1954)
Vendetta (1950)
Venetian Affair, The (1966)
V.I.P.s, The (1963)
Virginian, The (1946)
Virgin Queen, The (1955)
Viva Las Vegas (1964)

Wake Up and Dream (1946)
Wake Up and Live (1937)
Walk on the Wild Side, A (1962)
Wanted by the Police
Waterloo Bridge (1940)
Weekend at the Waldorf (1945)
We're Not Married (1952)
Westward the Women (1951)
We Who Are Young (1940)
What Nancy Wanted (1947)
Where Danger Lives (1964)
Where Were You When the Lights Went Out? (1968)
White Cargo (1942)
White Christmas (1954)
White Cliffs of Dover, The (1944)
Who's Afraid of Virginia Woolf (1966)
Wife, Doctor, and Nurse (1937)
Wife, Husband and Friend (1939)
Wife of Monte Cristo (1946)
Wild Blue Yonder, The (1951)
Will Success Spoil Rock Hunter? (1957)
Wings of the Navy (1947)
Winner Take All (1976)
Winning Team, The (1952)
Wizard of Oz, The (1939)
Woman Against Woman
Woman of Distinction, A (1950)
Women, The (1939)
Wonderful World of the Brothers Grimm, Th (1962)
Words & Music (1948)
World in His Arms, The (1952)
World Premiere (1941)
Wyoming Mail (1955)

Yankee Doodle Dandy (1942)
Yearling, The (1947)
Yellow Rolls Royce, The (1964)
Yolanda and the Thief (1945)
You for Me (1952)
Young and the Beautiful, The
Young at Heart (1955)
Young Bess (1953)
Young Doctor Kildare (1938)
Young Philadelphians, The (1959)
Yours for the Asking (1936)

Zaza (1939)
Ziegfield Girl (1941)
Ziegfield Follies (1947)

Following are some of the television series, programs, movies, and miniseries in which Joseff jewelry and props have appeared.

"Academy Awards, The"
"Alcoa Theater"
"Automan"

"Bad Seed, The"
"Banacek"
"Barnaby Jones"
"Barney Miller"
"Batman"
"Beau Gueste"
"Beauty and the Beast"
"Beneker"
"Betty Grable Show"
"Beverly Hills Cowgirl Blues"
"Black Widow"
"Blood Brothers"
"Bob Hope Specials"
"Breaking the Ice"
"Buy Accident"

"CBS Matinee"
"Charlie's Girls"
"Chevy Mystery Show"
"Chips"
"Clifford"
"Clipper Ship, The"
"Columbo"
"Commander Cody Series"
"Confidentially Yours"
"Cool Breeze"
"Crossings"
"Cyanide Touch"
"Cyd Charisse Show"

"Daddy - Mike Gannon"
"Danny Thomas Show"
"Deadly Key"
"Dealer's Choice"
"Dennis Day Show"
"Designing Women"
"Diamond Jim"
"Dinah Shore Show"
"Don Loper Fashion Show"
"Dragnet Dream West"
"Dukes of Hazard"
"Dynasty"

"Eddie Dodd"
"Ellery Queen"

"Elvis and Me"
"Emmy's, The"

"Falcon Crest"
"Family, The"
"Fantasy Island"
"F.B.I., The"
"Feather and Father"
"Fire on the Mountain"
"Flip Wilson Show, The"
"Flo Ziegfeld Story, The"
"Footnote on a Doll"
"Ford Startime"
"Fox Fire"
"Full House"

"Gemini"
"George Gobel Show, The"
"Get Christie Love"
"Girl with Something Extra"
"Goldie and the Boxer"
"Great Diamond Robbery"

"Hardy Boys, The"
"Harry and Rodger"
"Harry O"
"Hart to Hart"
"Hawaiian Eye"
"Headdress Ball"
"Henry West"
"Hiram Holiday"
"Hitchcock Presents"
"Hollywood Brat"
"Hotel"
"Houston Nights"
"Hunter"

"I Dream of Jeannie"
"If Tomorrow Comes"
"I Love Lucy"
"Invaders, The"
"Ironsides"

"Jack Webb Show"
"Jake and the Fatman"
"Jane Wyman Theatre, The"
"Jigsaw John"
"Joe Forrester"
"Juggler, The"

"Killer's Payoff"
"King of Diamonds"
"Knight Rider"
"Knot's Landing"
"Kojak"
"Kung Fu"

"Lady of the House"
"Land's End to Land's End"
"Little Miss Marker"
"Lost Hero"
"Love Boat, The"
"Loving Couples"
"Love's Savage Fury"

"Magnum P.I."
"Malice in Wonderland"
"Mannix"
"Man Who Found the Money"
"Markham"
"Matched Pearl, The"
"Matt Helm"
"Matt Houston"
"McMillan and Wife"
"Medical Center"
"Midnight Lace"
"Mike Hammer"
"Miss California Competitions"
"Mission Impossible"
"Money on the Side"
"Most Wanted"
"Moviola"
"Mr. Sunshine"
"Murder She Wrote"

"Necklace, The"
"Night Stalker"
"No Man's Land"
"Nutt House, The"

"Partridge Family, The"
"People Like Us"
"Petticoat Junction"
"Poker Alice"
"Police Woman"
"Private Resort"

"Queen for a Day"
"Quest"

"Ray Milland Show"
"Reckoning"
"Red Foxx Show, The"
"Remington Steele"
"RFK"
"Richie Brockelman"
"Rockford Files, The"
"Rogues, The"
"Rookies, The"
"Round Trip Mozambique"

"Sadat"
"Sanford and Son"
"Scarecrow and Mrs. King"
"Scared Silly"
"Schlitz Playhouse"
"Scruples "
"Secret of the Black Bayou"
"77 Sunset Strip"
"Shaft"
"Showboat"
"Sizzle"
"Sledge Hammer"
"Specialty of the House"
"Stand By Your Man"
"Story of Judith, The"
"S.W.A.T. "
"Switch"

"T.J. Hooker"
"Thriller, The"
"Torch Song Trilogy"
"Trader Horn"
"Trespass"
"Twilight Zone"
"Two Mrs. Grenvilles "

"Walter Winchell Show, The"
"Waltons, The"
"Webster"
"Winner Take All"
"Wonder Woman"

"Zorro"

Index

Adam's Rib, 69
Adventures of Don Juan, The, 94, 95
Affairs of Cellini, The, 19
Ah, Wilderness, 86
Aherne, Brian, 69
Alexander's Ragtime Band, 178
Algiers, 46
Ali Baba Goes to Town, 36
Allen, Woody, 11
Allyson, June, 50
Always Goodbye, 34, 83
Ameche, Don, 77
Anderson, Richard, 168
Anderson, Dame Judith, 179
Angel, Heather, 20
Annabel Takes a Tour, 55
Anthony Adverse, 28
Arch of Triumph, 37
Arkansas Travels, 139
Arnold, Edward, 77
Around the World in 80 Days, 173
Arrouge, Marty, 26
Arthur, Jean, 69
Astaire, Fred, 67
Astor, Mary, 58
Auntie Mame, 183

Bagdad, 97, 99
Baker, Kenny, 48
Ball, Lucille, 19, 36, 54, 55, 67, 104, 183
Bankhead, Tallulah, 60, 62, 104
Banton, Travis, 76
Barrymore, John, 10
Batman, 185
Bedtime Story, 59, 130
Bennett, Constance, 19, 123, 130, 147
Bergman, Ingrid, 37, 39
Berkley, Busby, 8
Bloom, Claire, 164
Blyth, Ann, 64, 165
Bogart, Humphrey, 44
Bond, Ward, 44
Born Yesterday, 169
Boyer, Charles, 46, 123
Bradna, Olympe, 35
Brennan, Owen, 115
Bride Wore Red, The, 123
Britton, Barbara, 26, 66
Bruce, Virginia, 58, 66
Buccaneer's Girl, 162

Cagney, James, 44
Call Me Madam, 182

Camille, 16, 19, 130
Cannon, Dyan, 183
Cantor, Eddie, 36
Carroll, Madeleine, 37
Carter, Janis, 64
Casbah, 46, 49, 172
Chaplin, Charlie, 104
Charisse, Cyd, 50
Churchill, Sir Winston, 68
Cimmaron, 16
Cleopatra, 184
Clift, Montgomery, 177
Cobb, Irvin, S, 33
Colbert, Claudette, 69
Coleman, Ronald, 38, 81
Collins, Joan, 185
Como, Perry, 50
Cooper, Gary, 8, 39, 69
Cooper, Gladys, 87, 88, 94
Corrigan, Lloyd, 64
Crawford, Joan, 69, 97, 104, 123, 163
Crawford, Broderick, 166, 169
Crews, Laura Hope, 18, 19
Crosby, Bing, 176
Cukor, George, 108
Curtis, Tony, 172, 183

Curtis, Jamie Lee, 50
Curtiz, Michael, 95

Dahl, Arlene, 79
Darnell, Linda, 60, 92, 93
Davis, Bette, 51, 69, 72, 74, 75, 82, 86, 90, 168
Day, Larraine, 147, 166
De Haviland, Olivia, 130, 140, 177
de Carlo, Yvonne, 49, 161, 172
Del Rio, Delores, 22
DeMille, Cecil B., 9
Denny, Reginald, 23
Desert Hawk, The, 161
Destry Rides Again, 167
Dexter, Anthony, 12, 22
Diamond Jim, 77
Dietrich, Marlene, 30, 81
Dodge City, 140
Don Juan, 10
Douglas, Melvyn, 38
Down to Earth, 92
Dowson, Ernest, 104
Dream Street, 10
Dreamboat, 174, 175
Dunne, Irene, 69, 123, 169
Durante, Jimmy, 51

Durbin, Deanna, 51, 58, 73, 123, 171
Dynasty, 185

Edison, Thomas, 7
Elvis and Me, 185
Emerson, Faye, 115
Everybody's Old Man, 33
Exile Express, 123

Fairbanks, Douglas, Jr., 11, 100, 140
Fan, The, 37
Farrell, Glenda, 130
Faye, Alice, 28, 60, 76, 77, 78, 123, 169
Fighting Guardsman, The, 64, 169
Fitzgerald, F. Scott, 107
Fleming, Rhonda, 173
Fleming, Victor, 107, 108
Flying Down to Rio, 16
Flynn, Errol, 94, 95
Fonda, Henry, 77
Fontaine, Joan, 83
Fools for Scandal, 58
Forever Amber, 60, 92, 93
Foster, Preston, 48
Francis, Kay, 22, 58, 73, 171
Fredericks, John, 107
Frenchie, 167, 169

Gable, Clark, 8, 63, 104, 107, 109, 110, 111, 123, 166
Gahagan, Helen, 38
Gallant Lady, 34
Garbo, Greta, 8, 17, 18, 83, 130
Gardner, Ava, 170
Garfield, John, 82, 90
Garland, Judy, 48, 50, 67
Garson, Greer, 80
Gay Divorcee, The 16
Gaynor, Janet, 86, 123
Gertie the Dinosaur, 8
Gibbons, Cedric, 16, 18
Gielgud, John, 164
Gigi, 38
Gilbert, John, 11
Goddard, Paulette, 104
Goldwyn, Samuel, 9
Gone With The Wind, 16, 38, 102-111
Grahame, Gloria, 52
Granger, Stewart, 179
Grant, Cary, 69, 83
Great Sinner, The, 170
Great Train Robbery, The, 8
Great Ziegfeld, The, 67
Greene, Richard, 161
Griffith, D. W., 8
Gunga Din, 140
Gwenn, Edmund, 88

Harlow, Jean, 8, 29, 69
Hart, Lorenz, 50
Harvey Girls, The, 48
Hayes, Helen, 107
Hayward, Susan, 86
Hayward, Louis, 26
Hayworth, Rita, 8, 58, 92, 99, 130, 178, 179, 180
Head, Edith, 163
Hecht, Ben, 108
Heflin, Van, 88
Heiress, The, 177
Hepburn, Katharine, 21, 42, 69, 91
High Society, 176
Hired Wife, 69
His Girl Friday, 69
Hitting a New High, 36
Hix, Ernest, 199, 159
Holliday, Judy, 169
Hollywood Canteen, 82
Hope, Bob, 147
Hopper, Hedda, 185
Horne, Lena, 67
Houston, Walter, 43
Hovick, Louise, 36
Howard, Sidney, 107, 108
Hubert, Rene, 37, 68
Hucksters, The, 166
Hudnut, Richard, 12
Hudnut, Winifred, 12
Hudson, Rochelle, 33
Hugo, Victor, 31

Hunchback of Notre Dame, The, 31

I Married a Communist, 166
If Winter Comes, 166
It Happened One Night, 123
It's a Date, 17, 73

Jazz Singer, The, 10
Jergens, Adele, 99
Jezebel, 69
Jungle Book, The, 84

Kelly, Grace, 176
Kelly, Gene, 50, 67, 99
Kerr, Deborah, 166
Keyes, Evelyn, 49, 146
Killer That Stalked New York, The, 49
King Kong, 139
King, Andrea, 79, 162
Kismet, 81
Knapp, Evelyn, 58, 148
Kobal, John, 24
Korda, Alexander, 68, 84

Lady Hamilton, 68
Lamarr, Hedy, 46, 96
Lamour, Dorothy, 163
Lanchester, Elsa, 167
Lane, Rosemary, 34, 44, 45, 83, 150
Lane, Lola, 150
Lane, Priscilla, 137, 150
Lang, June, 130
Lansbury, Angela, 48, 96, 98
Lasky, Jesse, 8
Lasky, Jesse, Jr., 9, 65
Laughton, Charles, 180
Laurie, Piper, 172
Le Roy, Mervyn, 58
Lee, Gypsy Rose, 36
Leigh, Vivian, 8, 32, 68, 104
Leigh, Janet, 50
Lemmon, Jack, 183
Leslie, Joan, 46, 165
Let's Live a Little, 53
Leventhal, Albert, 10
Libeled Lady, 29
Lights of New York, 10
Lillian Russell, 28, 76, 77, 78, 79, 169
Lindfors, Viveca, 94, 95
Little Egypt, 173
Little Women, 16
Lombard, Carole, 58, 69, 123
Look Who's Laughing, 55
Loos, Anita, 26
Lorre, Peter, 49
Lost Horizon, 96
Louise, Anita, 28, 169
Love Affair, 169, 123
Love Machine, The, 183
Loves of Carmen, The, 99
Loy, Myrna, 8, 29, 69, 72, 123
Lucas, Paul, 20
Lupino, Ida, 82

MacArthur, Charles, 107
MacDonald, Jeanette, 17, 94, 123
MacLaine, Shirley, 173
MacMurray, Fred, 69
Mad Miss Manton, The, 32
Magnificent Fraud, The, 56, 57
Malice in Wonderland, 185
Marie Antoinette, 23, 24, 25, 26, 155
Marriage is a Private Affair, 37
Martin, Tony, 36, 49
Mary of Scotland, 21, 73
Massey, Ilona, 37
Mature, Victor, 43
Mature, Victor, 84, 96
Maxwell, Marilyn, 86
Mayer, Louis B., 24, 104, 107
Mayo, Virginia, 146
McCoy, Winsor, 8
Menzies, William Cameron, 107
Mercer, Johnny, 48
Merman, Ethel, 182
Merton of the Movies, 52
Milland, Ray, 35
Minnelli, Vincent, 67
Miranda, Carmen, 181
Mitchell, Margaret, 103
Mix, Tom, 11

Monroe, Marilyn, 8, 183
Montez, Maria, 65
Moore, Constance, 134
Morgan, Dennis, 66, 79
Morning Glory, 16
Mourning Becomes Electra, 89
Mr. Peabody and the Mermaid, 64
Mrs. Miniver, 80
Mrs. Parkington, 87
Muni, Paul, 90
Munson, Ona, 43, 60
Murder She Wrote, 169
My Wild Irish Rose, 79

Nancy Goes to Rio, 181
New Mission Impossible, The, 62
Northwest Passage, 37
Nugent, Frank, 19, 107

O'Hara, Maureen, 31, 97, 99, 136
O'Neill, Eugene, 86
Oakie, Jack, 36
Oklahoma Kid, The, 44
Olcott, Chauncey, 79
Olivier, Lawrence, 68, 164

Page, Gale, 149
Parker, Eleanor, 13
Parker, Jean, 139
Parsons, Louella, 185
Patrick, Gail, 83, 129, 142
Paxinou, Katina, 89
Peck, Gregory, 170
People Like Us, 169
Perfect Marriage, The, 71
Philadelphia Story, The, 69, 176
Pickford, Mary, 8, 11, 162, 163
Pidgeon, Walter, 166
Pirates of Monterey, 65
Plunkett, Walter, 16, 19, 20, 21, 73, 103, 105, 107, 115
Pons, Lily, 36
Porter, Edwin S., 8
Powell, Jane, 181
Powell, William, 8, 29, 66, 69
Powell, William, 8, 29, 66, 69
Power, Tyrone, 13, 26, 72, 74
Presley, Priscilla, 185
Presley, Elvis, 185
Prince Who was a Thief, The, 172
Prisoner of Zenda, The, 38
Private Lives of Elizabeth and Essex, The, 69, 74, 75
Purple Rose of Cairo, The, 11

Quicksand, 66
Quinn, Anthony, 13, 74, 101

Rainer, Luis, 66
Rains, Claude, 90
Rains Came, The, 13, 72, 74
Rambova, Natasha, 12
Reagan, Ronald, 165
Reed, Donna, 88
Return of Monte Cristo, 26, 66
Rhodes, Leah, 39
Richard III, 164
Riddle of the Dangling Pearl, The, 39
Robin Hood, 130
Robinson, Ann, 153
Rodgers, Richard, 50
Rogers, Buddy, 162
Rogers, Ginger, 69, 140, 174, 175
Romanoff, Mike, 116
Romeo and Juliet, 8, 26
Rooney, Mickey, 50, 66
Roosevelt in Africa, 8
Roosevelt, Elliott, 115
Rose Marie, 94
Royal Scandal, A, 60
Royle, Edwin M., 9
Runyon, Damon, 166
Russell, Jane, 122
Russell, Rosalind, 42, 69, 73, 90, 123, 171

Sabu, 84
Salome, 178, 179, 180
Samson & Delilah, 84, 96
Sanders, George, 37
Saratoga Trunk, 39

Saxon Charm, The, 176
Say it in French, 35
Sea Hawk, The, 68
Sea of Grass, The, 91
Selig, William F., 8
Selznick, David O., 104
Selznick, Myron, 104
Shanghai Express, 30
Shanghai Gesture, 43, 60
She, 38
Shearer, Norma, 23, 24, 25, 26, 104, 123
Sheik, The, 12
Sheridan, Ann, 143
Shirley, Anne, 147
Sinatra, Frank, 176
Sinbad the Sailor, 13, 74, 100, 101
Siren of Atlantis, 65
Sisters, The, 86
Some Like it Hot, 183
Song of Bernadette, The, 87
Sons of the Musketeers, 94
Sothern, Ann, 181
Squaw Man, The, 9
Stanwyck, Barbara, 32, 34, 42, 83
Steiner, Max, 38, 108
Stella Dallas, 34
Sten, Anna, 53, 123
Sterling, Tisha, 181
Stevens, Mark, 173
Stop You're Killing Me, 166
Story of a Divorce, The, 51, 168
Summer Holiday, 86
Sutton, Kay, 71

Tamiroff, Akim, 56, 57
Taylor, Robert, 32
Taylor, Elizabeth, 184, 185
Temple, Shirley, 8
Thalberg, Irving, 16, 18, 26
That Night in Rio, 60
Thatcher, Heather, 58
There Goes my Heart, 58
Thin Man, The, 30, 69
This Time for Keeps, 51
Three Smart Girls Grow Up, 123
Three Musketeers, The, 20, 98, 99
Tierney, Gene, 43
Toren, Marta, 49
Totter, Audrey, 176
Tracy, Spencer, 29, 69, 163
Trent, Paul, 10
Trevor, Clair, 166
Turner, Lana, 37, 88, 98, 99

Up in Central Park, 51, 58

Vaccaro, Brenda, 169
Valentino, 12, 13
Valentino, Rudolph, 8, 12, 13, 72, 117
Van Druten, John, 107
Von Sternberg, Josef, 30

Wanted by the Police, 148
Waterloo Bridge, 33
Wayne, John, 8
Wheeler, Lyle, 108
Whitty, Dame May, 51
Wife, Doctor and Nurse, 130
Wife, Husband and Friend, 59
Wilson, Kathleen, 13, 138
Windsor, Kathleen, 92
Windsor, Marie, 169
Winters, Shelley, 167
Wood, Sam, 108
Woman of Distinction, A, 73, 171
Woman of the Year, 69
Women, The, 69, 97
Words and Music, 50
Wray, Fay, 31, 45, 139
Wycherly, Margaret, 99
Wyman, Jane, 47

Young, Loretta, 59, 71, 130
Young, Roland, 36

Zelle, Joy, 32
Ziegfeld Follies, 67

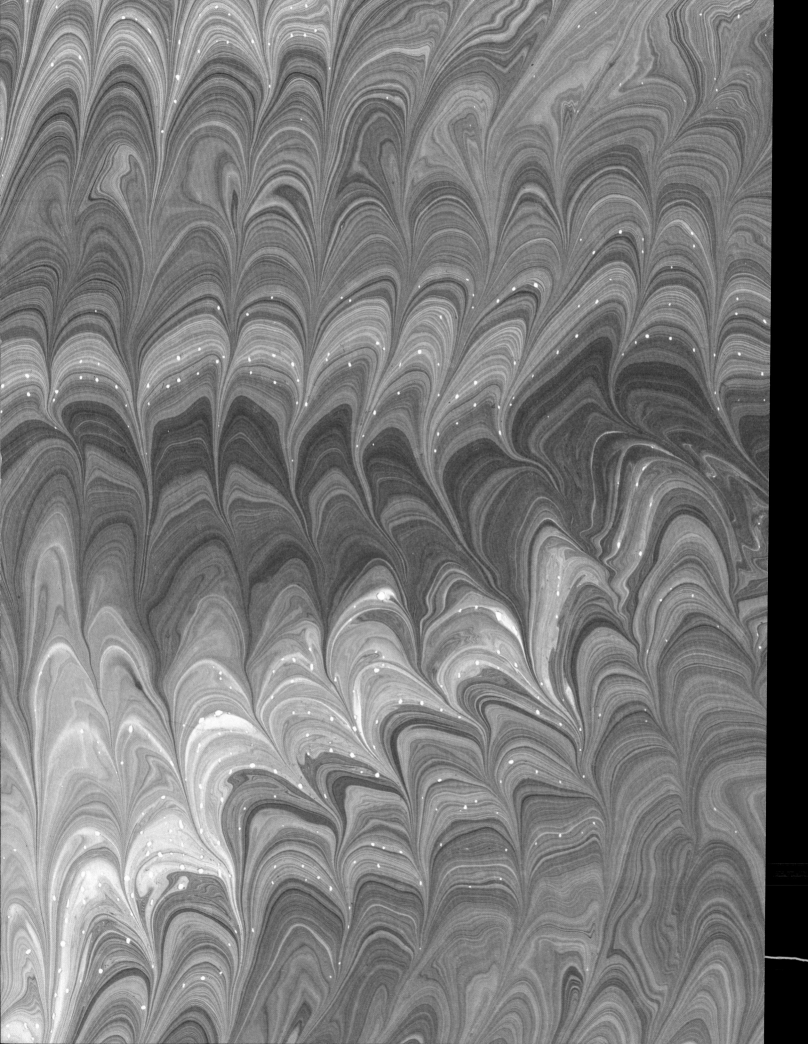

PRICE GUIDE

for retail jewelry in *Jewelry of the Stars*, Joanne Dubbs Ball . Schiffer Publishing © Copyright 1991. Values vary immensely according to the piece's condition, location of the market, and overall quality of design. While one must make their own decisions, we can offer a guide. All values listed are in U.S. dollars ($).

Page 127
Left to right:
necklace/earrings parure	$450-600
earrings (top)	150-200
brooch	200-350
pendant	150-225
bracelet	375-500
cupid earring	175-250
heart earrings	175-250
cupid brooch	375-550

Page 129
Bottom photo:
left top brooch	225-350
bottom brooch	650-850
chatelaine	600-750
brooch on photo, left	450-600
tassel brooch	500-650

Page 130
Top left brooch	300-400
Right necklace	500-600
Bottom left cross	450-600

Page 131
Top left necklace	400-500
Top right photo:	
acorn lariat	250-350
bell necklace	150-200
bib necklace	250-350
Bottom photo:	
mesh lariat	400-500
leaf choker	400-500
line necklace	275-350

Page 132
Top left photo:	
Mayan necklace	400-500
bracelets (each)	150-300
Top right photo:	
bar brooches	150-200 each
oval brooch	200-250
dangle brooch	225-275
"diamond" brooch	200-250
Bottom photo: left to right	
flower head brooch	200-300
lily of the valley brooch	300-400
orchid brooch	350-400
necklace	450-600
chain dangle brooch	450-600
tassel necklace	275-375
bouquet brooch	350-425
oval brooch	500-600

Page 133
Top: left to right	
square brooch	225-300
leaf brooch	250-350
grapes brooch	300-400
round brooch	150-200
crown brooch	200-300
peacock feathers	250-400

horsehead brooch	200-300
flower brooch	150-200
cluster brooch	375-500
Bottom photo:	
necklace & bracelet	650-800
necklace, center	400-500

Page 134
turban brooch	275-350

Page 135
top necklace	900-1200
bottom necklace	1000-1500

Page 136
Top left brooch	500-750
money tree brooch	600-800

Page 137
charm brooch	600-800
Bottom photo from top left:	
brooch	275-350
brooch	400-550
middle brooch	350-500
2-dangle brooch	500-700
bottom brooch	400-550
large brooch	800-950
3-dangle brooch	600-800

Page 138
Top photo:	
top necklace	2000-3000
bottom necklace	1500-2500

Page 139
Top right, necklace	500-600
Bottom photo:	
rings	350-600
brooch	800-950

Page 140
Top left cartouche	450-600
Top right photo:	
brooches	500-900
necklace	200-300
Bottom left pin	275-375

Page 141
Top left photo:	
top brooch	300-400
center brooch	350-450
bottom brooch	1000-1500
Right photo:	
top necklace	1500-2000
bottom necklace	1000-1200
Bottom photo:	
top brooch	500-650
bottom brooch	600-800

Page 142
Right photo:	
flowers	175-300 each
headhunters	500-700

Page 143
Bottom photo:	
top	450-550
bottom	550-650

Page 144
crab brooch	250-350
sun god brooch	150-250
turtle brooch	125-200
camel pendant	500-700
elephant necklace	850-1200

Page 145
Left photo:	
owl necklace	500-650
scarab necklace, earrings	1000-1500
Top right earrings	175-375 per pair

Page 146
Right seashell necklace	275-375

Page 147
Top left drum necklace	500-700
Right, key brooch	250-350

Page 148
Top, from left:	
necklace	600-700
brooch	300-400
pendant & 5 chains	500-650
circle & 4 chains	400-500
rectangle & 5 chains	450-600
round pendant	200-300
Bottom photo:	
astrological brooches	150-300 each

Page 149
Right photo:	
necklace	500-600
bracelet	300-400

Page 150
Top brooch	500-600

Page 152
Top photo:	
(top to bottom) oval	250-350
square	300-400
round	300-400
Bottom photo:	
(clockwise from top center)	
brooch	375-550
earrings	150-200
heart brooch	200-275
bracelet	375-500
necklace	250-325

Page 153
Set	850-1000

Page 154
Set	2000-2500